T-Hangar Tales

By

Joseph P. Juptner

HA Historic Aviation

T-Hangar Tales

By Joseph P. Juptner

Published as part of the
"HISTORIC AIRCRAFT SERIES"
HISTORIC AVIATION Publishers & Wholesalers
1401 Kings Wood Rd., Eagan, MN 55122-3811
612/454-2493
James B. Horne, Publisher

The "Historic Aircraft Series" is published to document the careers and service of the men and machines that gave America Wings. Other titles in this series from Historic Aviation are:

Piper: A Legend Aloft
by Edward H. Phillips

Beechcraft, Pursuit of Perfection
by Edward H. Phillips

Cessna, A Master's Expression
by Edward H. Phillips

Travel Air, Wings Over the Prairie
by Edward H. Phillips

Wings of Cessna, Model 120 to the Citation X
by Edward H. Phillips

Speed, the Biography of Charles Holman
by Noel Allard

The 91 Before Lindbergh
by Peter Allen

DH-88: The Story of DeHavilland's Racing Comets
by David Ogilvy

Of Monocoupes and Men
by John Underwood

The Stinsons
by John Underwood

Aircraft Service Manual Reprints
Piper J-3 Cub
Aeronca 7AC Champ
Aeronca 11AC Chief
Taylorcraft BC-12D
Ercoupe

Aircraft Flight Manual Reprints
F-51D Mustang
B-29 Superfortress

T-Hangar Tales

Publishers & Wholesalers
1401 Kings Wood Rd.
Eagan, MN 55122 U.S.A.

Library of Congress Cataloging in Publication Data
94-77950
Juptner, Joseph P.
T-Hangar Tales
Aviation history

ISBN 0-911139-18-4 Softcover

Printed and bound in the United States of America
Art Director, Noel Allard
Layout, James B. Horne
Typesetting, Cindy Reever
Cover Artist, Jo Kotula

DEDICATION

This work is dedicated to further the knowledge for those interested in perpetuating an awareness that is due also to the hundreds upon hundreds of bright-eyed entrepreneurs, eye-ball engineers, shade-tree mechanics, and the little-guy sportsmen pilots that also did their part in the advancement of aviation to the stature it now enjoys. Many had not the wherewithall, but they did have the spirit!

GREETINGS

This book is a hodge-podge of interesting data, stories, anecdotes, and very rare photographs, so-called "stuff" that one is not likely to find in any one book.

Just about all of the stories and information that are contained here were either researched over the years by the author, or related to him by people who were participants of the historic occasion or were just lucky enough to be there when it happened.

As stories, and even memories often will, some were perhaps embellished by happy times remembered or some fleeting "white-knuckle" experience.

Also, remembering things to the last detail was lost in the passage of time to become fuzzy and inexact.

But mostly, this is the way that things were.

T-Hangar Tales

Hangar-flying, probably as old as aviation itself, was something airplane people would do on those days when it was impossible to go aloft, or after the day's flying had ended. Hangar-flying could be accomplished either grouped around congenially in a hangar, under the wing of a parked airplane, in an operations shack, or even at the airport restaurant. In this way many pleasant hours, often hilarious hours, would be spent sitting among those of your kind. If one was to measure the gist of what was being said, almost everything could be categorized as information or lessons learned. There was a lot to learn to being a success in earlier aviation, and what one could learn from others in this vast and exciting arena was most always useful and timely.

Of course there were true stories, tall tales, and yarns of bravado. Escapades, too, that were often exaggerated in the re-telling, but they most always were basic fact; fact that was only sometimes stretched a little for laughs. So, if you had just got back from Ohio, or Georgia, or Michigan, and some fellows there were building this sporty little cabin monoplane for two that was sure to be a hit, you would tell your friends, and that's how news got around. Also, if you needed a "Crank" or a "jug" for your engine, a Bendix 30 x 5 wheel, or even a better "prop," someone could surely put you on to a good deal they happened to run across along the way.

Being a clannish bunch, often living on the edge of poverty, or disaster, early-day pilots gravitated towards one another, and were quick to go where they were welcome. As pilots traipsed around the countryside, whether on whim or purpose, they tended to look one another up — perhaps to share a recent experience, trade the latest gossip, or swap some tid-bids of valuable information. It was in this way that the aviation-community knew what was going on around them. It was handy to bone-up, too, on who was building or rebuilding what, who was hiring, what was up for sale and where, and often a fellow could get steered to where a good craftsman or a good pilot could make a decent buck or two.

Over the years, especially the two decades of fantastic progress prior to World War II, hangar-flying had now become a national ritual that was certainly pleasant, often the creator of lasting friendships, and nearly always was enlightening and very educational. If you've never had the pleasure of attending a "hangar-flying session," by all means do try it; you will enjoy the experience, and it is sure to broaden your knowledge about many things!

Joseph P. Juptner

ACKNOWLEDGEMENTS

The following good-hearted people made a book like this possible: George Townson, Martin Cole, Earl C. Reed, Charles W. Meyers, Stephen J. Hudek, Gerald Deneau, "Lou" Tipper, Charlie Morris, H. Lloyd Child, Theron K. Rhinehart, Louis M. "Tex" Lowry, W. U. Shaw, Dave Stevenson, C. G. Taylor, "Bob" Pickett, James Bott, and Alfred V. Verville.

PHOTO CREDITS

Alexander Aircraft Co., Charles W. Meyers, Earl C. Reed, Winstead Brothers, Caterpillar Tractor Co., Smithsonian National Air Museum, Stephen J. Hudek, Cessna Aircraft Co., Peter M. Bowers, Sikorsky Aircraft Division, Fairchild-Hiller Co., H. Lloyd Child, Emil Strasser, Robert S. Hirsch, Louis M. "Tex" Lowry, W. U. Shaw, Roy Oberg, Marion Havelaar, North American Aviation, and of course, Gerald H. Balzer who was the most generous!

Edith Foltz had to leave her dog at home!

Dapper, young, Edith Foltz was an accomplished aviatrix from Portland, Oregon. Showing promise, she was coached for this coming race by "Tex" Rankin and tutored to fly this revolutionary low-winged Alexander "Bullet" in the very first "Woman's Air Derby." Promoters and hordes of reporters had a field day with this event because of its "ad" value. It was not long before it came to be popularly known as the "Powder Puff Derby!" In among the other scheduled events, this was a new race, and more-or-less a trial run from Santa Monica, California to Cleveland, Ohio, where the week-long National Air Races for 1929 were being held.

The long cross-country derby, with no precedent to go by, turned out to be quite a grueling contest for the eager lady-pilots. Because of varying degrees of experience, some had varying degrees of problems. Several even got lost along the way, and there were even a few mishaps; some were slight and some quite serious. In drawing on her talent, and probably taking advantage of some luck too, Miss Foltz, our heroine, finished in second place to the veteran Phoebe Omlie in the "CW" class. Experienced and determined, "Phoebe" was setting a fast pace in her (110 h.p.) Warner-powered "Monocoupe Special." A veteran at this kind of flying, she stayed well ahead of the pack (in class) throughout the race. Newspapers across the country kept up a running account daily of the ladies' progress, and high-lighted every little incident.

The race-for-the-ladies, in many ways, was a huge success, but the second-place win by Miss Foltz was later disputed by two other lady-pilots. Several accounts reporting the official race results do credit Miss Foltz with coming in second, in class, and thus it was scored.

Lest this ditty seem like just a routine account of some bygone air-race, the sole reason for this tale was a ridiculous and comical twist-of-fate that was not all that funny to Edith Foltz! The dog (a German Shepherd), shown sitting in the airplane, was a beloved pet, and Edith proposed to take the well-behaved animal along for company on the long cross-country trip to Cleveland, Ohio. But, according to the all-knowing race officials, to whom rules were set in concrete, she would not be allowed to take her pet along. Because, right there in black and white the air-race rules strictly specified "no males would be allowed to go along, or to participate in this contest!" Her four-legged friend, you see, could not go along, or to participate, because he was "a male dog!" *(Photo from Alexander Aircraft Co.)*

Edith Foltz on her way to Cleveland!

KELLETT K - 2 AUTOGIRO - CONTINENTAL A-70

"The Autogiro!"

A chance helicopter flight some years ago was so intriguing it instigated a hangar-flying session about rotary-winged airplanes. Since the "Autogiro" was in its hey-day some 60 years ago it is not surprising how vaguely it is remembered. Some old-timers do remember the special antics of the autogiro very clearly, but to most it is a mystery out of the past. Usually called "giro," or even paddle-plane, it is surely worth a bit of discussion about its development and what it contributed to the science of aeronautics.

Briefly, the autogiro differs from normal fixed-wing airplanes in the source of its lifting capacity; its total lift was created by freely-rotating airfoiled blades. Supporting rotation was independent of the engine, and rotation was only produced by air pressure that was caused by movement of the giro in any direction. Yes, in any direction, be it climbing, gliding, in level flight, or in steep descent. The engine's only function was to propel the machine forward. Take-offs were quick, snappy, and short; steep climb-out was even possible immediately to clear any obstacles ahead. Theoretically and in practice, the design principles were such that any obstacle the giro could not clear safely, it could land again safely in front of!

Level flight speeds were up to 100 m.p.h. or better, or as slow as 25 m.p.h. with perfect control; it was even possible to hover for a moment or two. Slow-speed flight, even in a banked turn was no hazard. (Try that in a fixed-wing airplane.) The normal glide was very slow, providing ample time in the selection of an emergency landing area. Near-vertical descent with very little forward speed was less than that of a man coming down in a parachute. Very near fool-proof, as compared to fixed-wing airplanes, the giro could be flown quite safely with normal operating skills, but it still required a superb flying technique to bring out its fullest performance capabilities. We are talking about an overall performance that was actually amazing when done right!

Shown here popping off the mat and grabbing altitude is the Kellett model K-2. Seating two side-by-side, it was powered with a seven cylinder Continental A-70 engine of 165 h.p., and was a versatile flying machine of some unusual abilities. The price-tag of $7885 slanted the K-2 at the well-heeled business man, or the sportsman-pilot. But alas, there were not many of these well-heeled business men or sportsman-pilots around during the hard times of 1931-32-33. Offered in several other versions, the Kellett finally reached its peak of development just before World War II, and then quietly faded from the scene. A thing out of the illustrious past, the "autogiro" concept could perhaps still make a place for itself even today! *(A Fred Hess & Son photo from collection of Gerald H. Balzer.)*

KELLETT K-3 - KINNER C5

A Kellett K-3 high over Los Angeles.

FEDERAL CM-3 - 1928-29 - 7 CYL HALLETT

Federal Aircraft CM-3.

Among the many airplanes that were designed and built needlessly in California during the 1928-29 season was the nondescript Federal CM-3. As the story goes in hangar-talk, a group of enterprising airplane mechanics (from the former Ryan Mechanics Monoplane Co.) wheedled some financing here and there, and proposed to continue in the seemingly, lucrative business of building airplanes for the civil market. Becoming the Federal Aircraft Corp. in Los Angeles during February of 1928, they employed William J. Waterhouse to engineer their craft for approval, and then moved to facilities in San Bernardino, California. As shown, the CM-3 was rolled out early in 1929 as a three-place (in tandem) sport monoplane. It was very average overall, and was powered with a seven cylinder Hallett engine of 130 h.p. This odd-ball engine was a pretty good fit for this odd-ball airplane. The listed flyaway price was to be $7000. They unashamedly claimed a backlog of a 50-plane order from nation-wide distributors, but the airplane shown was apparently the only CM-3 ever built! No doubt the project was scrubbed (mid 1929) and everybody abandoned ship when the money ran out. *(Photo from Gerald H. Balzer Collection.)*

Chinese people of the 1930s must have been more air-minded than any people could possibly be. In fact, they liked to fly so well that when CNAC put on hi-speed Douglas DC-2 airliners, which cut flying time in half on a route to famous cities and resorts, people complained loudly and stayed away in droves. When someone finally asked, an old sage explained that by traveling twice as fast the people missed half of the flying! Yes, and sound-proofed cabins were a nuisance too because you couldn't "hear the flying." So, would they please go back to using the slow and noisy Ford "Tri-Motors" — please!

"Centurian" by Century Aircraft.

The many-sided "Centurion" was at times called "Beal's Beauty" (apparently meaning Ralph Beal of Kansas City, Mo.). This was told by Earl C. Reed, one who knew most of the doings around both of the Kansas Cities prior to, and long after 1929. Like many other craft of this particular time, the ship remained experimental, and was never approved by the government in any category. "Wes" Hoag flew it most often, usually out of the Raytown, Missouri airport. Later, it was also flown out of the Harrisonville, Missouri airport, and was still reported to be flying well into the late 1930s. Except for its odd fuselage and cabin geometry, the airplane was otherwise quite normal. The tight-fitting NACA engine cowl was offered as an optional feature, but they say the airplane actually flew just as well without it!

A cabin monoplane seating three (pilot in front and two in back), the "Centurion" was powered with the new seven cylinder LeBlond 90 (7D) engine of 90 h.p. The ship's dimensions and aerodynamic proportions were quite similar to other airplanes of this type, but it did have a few little quirks of its own. Mainly the "greenhouse" cabin, and the tightly-cowled nose section. 'Tis said the plane was blessed with pretty good performance, and a fairly stout airframe. It was constructed of mixed materials as was the custom at this (1928-29) time. The "Centurion" was manufactured by the Century Aircraft Co. at Kansas City, Mo. Price was listed as $4975 at the factory. Scanning records, it is doubtful if any more than the one prototype (X-559E) was ever built. But then, according to Earl Reed himself, "it had been reported" that perhaps as many as nine examples were built, and scattered about Kansas and Missouri. *(Photo from Gerald H. Balzer Collection).*

PIETENPOL AIR CAMPER - 1931 - FORD MODEL A

"Bernie" Pietenpol builds an "Air Camper."

Like a good many other young men of modest means in the late 1920s and 1930s, mechanically-minded "Bernie" Pietenpol of Spring Valley, Minnesota found it difficult to afford flying. He did want to fly in an airplane of his own, but couldn't afford to keep up the average production-airplane that was up for sale at that time. Having in mind something smaller, simpler, and cheaper to operate, Pietenpol decided to design and build his own airplane. He fiddled with several designs before coming up with the happy-medium "Air Camper" in 1928.

Although relatively crude and old-fashioned by comparison, his two-seated "Air Camper" proved rugged and reliable with a built-in bonus of simplicity both in construction and in operation. Using a modified four cylinder water-cooled Ford "Model A" automobile engine of some 40 h.p. provided no great surge of performance, but it was adequate. The whole airplane, its maintenance and its operation was absolutely a tinkerer's delight! It first flew in 1929. Using the old "Eiffel 36" air-foil, the ship could get in and out of just about anywhere. The 1933 and subsequent models had been upgraded a little, but they were still the epitome of simplicity and just bare necessities. Twenty-three of the "Pietenpol" were registered in 1933.

After being featured in "Modern Mechanics" of 1930 as an airplane that just about anyone could build, the "Air Camper" (a catchy name) was being put together by many enthusiasts from the plans published in the magazine! Soon, many examples were seen flying all over the country from small-town airstrips and suitable pasture airports. It is fair to say that the relative success and down-home popularity of the "Pietenpol" stimulated others into constructing their own home built airplanes. A veritable rash of similar designs soon followed.

When government restrictions on unlicensed airplanes were finally enforced in the late 1930s, all of this activity was virtually put to rest. It was not until the 1950s that the home-built movement began to surface once more, and "Air Camper" plans were again on sale. Of course, in more recent years home-builders were incorporating modern niceties and techniques into the "Air Camper," but it is still basically the airplane of 60 some years ago! The examples that are still flying, here and there, are a tribute to the audacity of one Bernard H. Pietenpol. *(Photo from Gerald H. Balzer Collection.)*

LAIRD BABY BIPLANE - 1913 - HOFER 12 H.P.

"Mattie" Laird and "Baby Biplane" circa 1913.

One could hardly believe that the crude airplane shown here is a "Laird" biplane, but a fella has gotta start somewhere. Teaching himself to fly (well, sort of) in 1912, "Mattie" Laird built his second airplane in 1913 at the age of 17! Laird #2 as shown here with George "Buck" Weaver on the left, and E.M. "Mattie" Laird on the right was called the "Baby Biplane." Powered with a four cylinder, air-cooled "Hofer" engine of 12 h.p. it soon proved that young Laird was a whiz at getting pretty good performance with engines of low power. By 1915, "Mattie" had become quite proficient as a pilot, and began exhibition flying in the "Baby Biplane" on the "Fair Circuit" around the Midwest. He was finally flying for pay! Laird had built his fourth airplane in 1916, and with it he finally became known as an accomplished airplane-builder and exhibition flier. What followed after this period in his life is a remarkable story. *(Photo from Charles W. Meyers Collection.)*

ARROW SPORT PURSUIT - KINNER K-5

Traveling salesman makes calls by airplane!

As can be seen from the terrain underneath this "Arrow Sport," we are over the farm-belt in the mid-western plains of our U.S.A. This enterprising fellow flying the "Sport" is a farm-supplies and equipment salesman that used to make his rounds by automobile like everyone else. But that took up a lot of his time, and his daily contacts were few. With the airplane he could land on just about anyone's farm to pay a visit, to write up an order, or deliver small items that would fit along-side him in the cozy cockpit.

Large, bulky orders still had to be shipped by rail-freight, and the farmers had to pick up their shipments at the railroad depot, but they didn't mind. They did, after all, have better and more frequent contact with the salesman when he came by air. The farmers enjoyed the innovative service, they thought it was fun, and it was a break in their normal routine. His "Arrow Sport" as shown here was a two-place open cockpit biplane powered with a five cylinder Kinner K5 engine of 100 h.p. It couldn't carry all that much, but it was ideal for short hops, and getting in and out of farmer's pastures. *(Photo from Gerald H. Balzer Collection.)*

Back in 1937, Al and Les were two pilots from Kansas who owned an OX-5 powered "American Eagle" as partners. They both loved to fly, but they could never agree on who would be boss! Finally, in heated disagreement, Les took the engine, fuselage, and landing gear, while Al took the wings, tail group, and propeller. Thus it was until they settled the issue. Many more partners have felt the same way, but lacked initiative to do it!

FLEET BIPLANE - 1930 - KINNER

Paul Mantz sets outside-loop record!

"Fearless Freddie" Lund, well-known daredevil-pilot, flying a Waco "Taper-Wing" performed the first outside-loop (1928) ever made in a commercial airplane. This was a significant achievement because the outside-loop imposes a great negative strain on the airplane, the engine, and the pilot. Not every pilot, nor every airplane can do this maneuver safely. Whetted by the challenge, Charles "Speed" Holman in his special Laird LC-R200 biplane came along soon after and did two of the heretofore dreaded outside-loops! Then some young fellow (Billie Leonard) in a Warrior-powered Hess "Argo" biplane also did two, and so it went. "Tex" Rankin, aerobatic maestro, was doing air-shows (early 1930) in his "Great Lakes" biplane. He elected to show off his prowess, as usual, and did 19 of the negative-loops, one after the other, for a new record. Of course, all records are made to be broken, so hot-shot pilots would take a crack at the record, now and then. Some broke it, some not.

Paul Mantz, noted Hollywood stunt-pilot, who had done just about every trick and stunt imaginable for the "movies," reckoned he could beat the current outside-loop record. And, maybe run up enough of the "loops" so the record would stand for a while. Shown here taking off (July 1930) in his Kinner-powered "Fleet" biplane, he is gaining altitude for his assault on the record. He had plenty of well-wishers, and watchers, who would provide verification. Before the afternoon was over he had pushed over for 49 gut-wrenching loops. But, three were disqualified so he settled for 46!

Meanwhile, young Dorothy Hester (protogé of "Tex" Rankin) in a "Great Lakes" biplane, also made 46 of the outside-loops for a women's record. Later, she increased her record to 76 of the loops. "Tex" Rankin, who actually coached Miss Hester in her record attempt, felt compelled to go up and try again. This time he stayed up in his "Great Lakes" until he had done 131 of the blasted things! Was this the end of it — well, no. When Paul Mantz heard of this, he climbed into his "Fleet" again, and before he came back down he had made 146 of the outside-loops. This count surely must have discouraged any more fool-hardy attempts on his record. Some say the record still stands! Knowing Paul Mantz and his cool confidence in his ability, it is quite likely that had anyone beaten his record, he would have been obliged to go up and get it back. *(Photo from Gerald H. Balzer Collection.)*

ST. LOUIS CARDINAL - GENET 80

This "Cardinal" was a taxi to a gold mine.

Blaine Tuxhorn's Flying Service was one of the busiest in the Kansas City area for years. His apron buzzed with activity and his hangars bulged with all sorts of interesting airplanes. One of these was a St. Louis "Cardinal" that caught the eyes of many because it mounted a "Genet" engine. The five cylinder "Genet" was a British engine imported to this country by Fairchild. One could see something odd about this engine right away. The "prop" turned the wrong way! It was odd to see someone flip the prop from the wrong side.

This ship was first a C2-60 (LeBlond 5D-65) and then converted with the 80 h.p. "Genet" for high-altitude flying. Used as a rental for a time, it was sold to Dr. F. M. Planck. The doctor used it to fly to Colorado to see about his gold-mine holdings. Later in its life the "Cardinal" was converted again — this time with an 85 h.p. LeBlond 5DF engine. Registered -903K for serial #105 — its final disposition is unknown. *(An Earl C. Reed photo.)*

Crawford's motorized glider.

Back in the "Thirties," just after the aircraft market had its stilts kicked out from under it, many airplane manufacturers resorted to building simple low-cost primary gliders. It is hard to recall just who really started this new trend, but for a time you could buy one ready-made, or knock-down from Detroit Aircraft, Alexander, Cessna, Waco, or a dozen others. All were hoping to cash in on the nationwide fever!

Glider clubs had sprung up like a rash all over the country, and literally thousands of young-bloods were getting a chance to take to the air. Actually, only for a minute or two at a time, but at least cheaply. On a nice weekend, just about anywhere, you could see these gliders being slung-off an appropriate hillside, or being towed into flight by someone's "Model A" Ford. It was a heckuva lot of fun for everyone, but it was a good bit of work for the amount of flying-time that one could get in a day's time!

They have said that necessity was the mother of invention, and that is true, but leave it to the man who is also lazy, to come up with the best ideas. Now, it's not to say that William "Bill" Crawford of Seal Beach, California was all that lazy, but he did figure out an easier way to make a primary glider fly for more than just a few minutes!

The Henderson motorcycle engine was ever-popular as a powerplant for amateur flying-machines. Our hero mounted one of these into the frame of a primary glider, and there you are. The mating was comical and rather contraptionish, but it did save a lot of running around. Now flights were extended to the time the "Henderson" kept running! *(Winstead Brothers Photo.)*

CROSLEY MOONBEAM - 1928-29 - WARNER 110

Crosley builds a "Moonbeam."

Powell Crosley, Jr. made a fortune in radios and refrigerators, but he didn't fare so well in the airplane-building business. Very enthusiastic about airplanes, Crosley owned several, and dabbled in various facets of the budding industry. With airplane-building fever in high pitch during 1928-29 Crosley decided to enter the fray. Harold Hoekstra, a young aero-engineer from Michigan was engaged, and the first model to come out of the Crosley shop in Cincinnati, Ohio was the lovely "Moonbeam" as shown. Designed for sport and all-purpose service the handsome craft was a trim parasol monoplane that seated three in open cockpits. Stout of frame with a strong wing, the machine did fairly well with the seven cylinder Warner "Scarab" engine of 110 h.p. But, it really took the five cylinder Wright (R-540) J6 engine of 165 h.p. to put a little pep in its behavior. Drastic events that came about in 1929 stifled further development, and this "Moonbeam" was built only in the one prototype.

When "Aeronca" and the "Cub" brought a little life back into the airplane business, Crosley tried again with the "Flea," but it fizzled out also. Later on Hoekstra designed another "Moonbeam," this time a two-seated sport biplane. Crosley finally came to realize that airplanes were indeed much harder to sell than radios, or "Shelva-Dor" refrigerators; so, he shut the airplane plant down. Hoekstra later got on at Stinson Aircraft. In 1947, the little Crosley "Cobra" engine was paired with the first Mooney "Mite." Great things were predicted for this combination; development problems peculiar to using an "auto engine" in an airplane produced many set-backs. Powell Crosley, Jr. saw his airplane-building business become more hobby than business! *(Photo from Gerald H. Balzer Collection.)*

"Caterpillar" tractor as an airport tug??

A "Caterpillar" tractor with surface-defiling cleats in use as an airport tug? Surely, this must have been some eager ad-man's tongue-in-cheek set-up to promote the sale of more "Caterpillar" tractors. Set-up or not, the incident is shown here on the Swan Island airport in Portland, Oregon. The "airliner" being gassed up is the famous Fokker F-10-A "Super Tri-Motor" in the livery of the West Coast Air Lines which served routes up and down the western coast. As to the tractor, they had to be kidding! (Photo from Caterpillar Tractor Co.)

An early instance of aircraft noise as a nuisance was reported to the Postmaster General on 21 January 1928. The complaint came from the owner-operator of the Cackle Corner Poultry Farm of Garretsville, Ohio. The angry operator complained that noisy low-flying airplanes were scaring the dickens out of his chickens! And, disrupting their normal egg production. A stern letter of warning from the Post Office was forwarded to National Air Transport (NAT) who operated the New York to Chicago airmail route, suggesting strongly they fly higher, especially when over Garretsville, Ohio.

BUDD BB1 PIONEER AMPHIBIAN - 1930-31 - KINNER C5-210

Budd "Pioneer" was of stainless steel!

The pioneering Budd Amphibian, aptly called "Pioneer," was based on the Savoia-Marchetti S-56 design. It was the first stainless-steel airplane. Built in 1930-31 by Edward G. Budd Manufacturing Co. of Philadelphia, it was fashioned to demonstrate the practicality of the electrical shot-weld process in fabrication of stainless-steel assemblies for aircraft. After its successful maiden flight, it was flown well over 1000 hours on a tour throughout the U.S.A. This was to promote the use of stainless-steel in airplane structures. Later, it was shipped to Europe making an extensive tour throughout many countries. Several countries showed interest in the use of stainless-steel, and especially in the "shot-weld" process. Returning from the European tour, the "Pioneer" was partly uncovered to show its internal structure. In 1936, it was placed outdoors on exhibit. Exposed to all sorts of weather, it was left on exhibit for many years to prove the durability of stainless-steel as construction material for aircraft.

As a prototype airplane using stainless-steel for its entire structure, the "Pioneer" ended up much heavier than the standard S-56. It had to be powered with the big five cylinder Kinner C5 engine of 210 h.p. to bolster its performance. The airplane was made entirely of stainless-steel except for its wing cover which was airplane-grade cloth. A stainless-steel wire cloth was tried as cover, but there was no practical way to get it taut! The "Pioneer" model BB-1 was registered as NR-749N for serial #1; it was the only one of its kind. It is remarkable that the structure was exposed to all sorts of torture for over 40 years and showed no signs of decay! It was still on display as of May, 1980. Lessons learned in building the BB-1 were later used to manufacture the "Conestoga" transport. *(Photo from Gerald H. Balzer Collection.)*

Dr. Cross acquires a "Twin."

A little-known product under the "American Eagle" label was the special two-motored "Twin" designed and built especially for Dr. Walter Cross early in 1929. Dr. Cross was chief chemist for the (Kansas City, Missouri) Public Water Works, and also an avid aviation enthusiast. The good Doctor financed this (A-529) project out of his "kitty" for a lavish personal airplane. He wanted an airplane that would incorporate roomy comfort with twin-engined safety, and yet in a medium size that would allow him the utmost in day-in and day-out utility. Economy of operation was a factor too.

Designed mostly by Jack E. Foster with an over-the-shoulder assist by Dr. Cross, of course, construction methods of the boxy twin-tailed "Twin" were rather conventional for this period. But it did show signs of being designed and built perhaps in too big a hurry. The deep fuselage was basically a welded steel-tube structure that was faired to shape and covered in fabric. Upon this structure was mounted a fabric-covered 47 foot wooden built-up wing. The wing bracing trusses were made up to provide mounting points for the two engines and also the landing gear.

By contrast, the unwieldy configuration was somewhat out of the ordinary, for this period in time, at least. The pilot and sometimes a co-pilot, sat high up front in a drafty open cockpit. Here, they could watch the two nine cylinder (125 h.p.) Ryan-Siemens engines flex and shake in their mounts; but, the engines were well-muffled to hold down the noise. The enclosed cabin under the wing, described as roomy, could seat up to four in various arrangements including a couch. But, visibility out was rather dodgy and skimpy.

Flight tests in the dead of winter were continually greeted with various aggravations. The under-powered "Twin" was cranky at times, and said to be unfriendly when it did fly. It is not known who piloted the craft on its maiden flight, but it was veteran-flier Charlie Toth who was singled out as personal pilot for Dr. Cross. During repeated tests to get familiar with the airplane Toth managed to literally "crack it up" in a ground accident. He bent it up pretty badly. It laid around for a while never being rebuilt, and perhaps that's just as well. Most of the facts in this story were offered by old-time pilot Earl Reed who at the time was practically "family" at the "American Eagle" plant. *(Photo from Smithsonian National Air Museum.)*

DIABLO SPORT - 1930 - ANZANI 35 HP

Diablo Sport . . . a cute little devil!

What is so striking about this little cloud-buster is the fact that the designer went back, way back, perhaps to fashion a revival of the thrilling days of the "Great War." Can any red-blooded pilot look at this airplane pictured here, and not envision himself taking off in the early-morning mist on a "dawn patrol" with perhaps the chance of meeting the dreaded "Red Baron" in mortal combat! It is not known who designed this little airplane, but you can tell he fancied whimsy! As the "Diablo Sport" it was built in Stockton, California by the Diablo Aircraft Company in 1928-29. It's a good bet if plans were available now, it would be a devilish project for the so-called home builder. With no data to go by, it appears to be a single-seater, and is powered with a three cylinder (French) Anzani engine of about 35 h.p. The "Sport" was registered X-807M (as serial #1) and it appeared on the register in 1929. *(Photo from Gerald H. Balzer Collection.)*

FLEET MODEL 1 BIG TAIL - WARNER 110

The big tails were ruining the "Fleet's" figure!

The popular "Fleet" trainer had been ramblin' around the countryside in droves for years. It was an off-spring of the "Husky" series built by Consolidated Aircraft for the U. S. Navy. The "Fleet" was a tough, and thoroughly likeable airplane, but in time had built up a reputation of being a "killer" during a "tail-spin." For a while, all of the "Fleet" were prohibited from "intentional spins" for this reason, but this edict did not help all that much. During pilot training, as practiced in the 1930s, some did fall off into "involuntary spins" and not every one of these pulled out safely. For a while, too, the statistics were rather grim, and this became a popular subject in "hangar-flying sessions" at nearly every airport. There were even pilots that were downright afraid to go up in the "Fleet." So, used "Fleet" airplanes were up for sale everywhere, and selling pretty cheap.

The culprit that set off this problem was the big "lifting stabilizer" that in some attitudes would "blank off" the comparatively small fin and rudder that the "Fleet" came with. This, of course, caused inadequate recovery forces to stop the "spin." Some knowledgeable airplane fixer-uppers, like Earl Reed for instance, welded up vertical fins and rudders of more adequate area that applied the proper force to stop the rotation, and the "dreaded spin" was licked. The modification as shown here in one form was approved after tests, and it lifted all restrictions against "intentional spins." In sorting through stacks of photos, one can find many shapes that were devised for this purpose. Some were quite ugly and ruined the "Fleet's" nice figure, but they all did the job. All "Fleet" after the Model 7 came out with proper tail-groups right from the factory. *(Photo from Earl C. Reed.)*

"Lee Monoplane" by Eyerly.

This trim little damsel out of the Northwest was the "Lee Monoplane" by Lee Eyerly. Being of the long-held opinion, no doubt, that pilot and passengers should not sit together, Lee placed the pilot to the rear in an open cockpit where he could operate undisturbed. The two passengers sat in a chummy cabin area down in front where they could not pester the pilot. But, they could console one another that everything was going to be O.K. Well shaped and neatly built, the "Eyerly" was a rather handsome airplane, and a credit to the students of the "aero school" that put it together.

Powered with a seven cylinder Siemens-Halske SH-14 (German) engine of 97 h.p., the ship was said to have good performance and characteristics inherent to this type of design. In other words, a pretty good little airplane. It was also available with the five cylinder Kinner K5 engine of 90-100 h.p. for comparable performance. Classed as an "experimental," the "Lee Monoplane" was never submitted for government approval; it was basically a training exercise for Eyerly students to learn the ins and outs of designing and building an airplane. Manufactured by Eyerly School of Aeronautics at the Salem Airport in Salem, Oregon. *(Photo from Gerald H. Balzer Collection.)*

Something you're not likely to hear about nowadays; back in 1935, a very busy plant-manager was enticed into learning to fly. But, soon he found he couldn't afford the time to commute back and forth to the airport. So, the accommodating instructor offered to teach him during lunch-hour from a hay-field just next to the factory! Hard times such as those, even in 1935, could spur one to all sorts of genius!

HESS BLUEBIRD MISS WANDA - 1927 - WHIRLWIND J5C

"Bluebird" tries for New Zealand.

The formidable-looking machine pictured here is the Hess "Bluebird," an early design that came out of Wyandotte, Michigan. The Hess Brothers apparently built only four of this type. The last one was built early in 1927 with the Wright "Whirlwind" J5C engine for Captain Fred Giles. As reports say, Giles had planned to be an entry in the infamous "Dole Derby" to Honolulu, but was plagued with last-minute gremlins, and didn't get to the starting line in time. His plans, had he made it to Hawaii, were to continue on across the Pacific Ocean to New Zealand as a goodwill flight from America!

Later, when everything was in good order, Giles flew the ship (named "Wanda") to Mills Field in San Francisco from Wyandotte to prepare for the great over-water hop. On 22 November 1927, Giles took off and headed for Hawaii, but only got about 20 miles out and had to turn back — the ocean fog was just too deep and too dense to penetrate. Besides, he got disoriented in the heavy fog, fell into a "spin" and all his maps including the sextant flew out of the cockpit! Luckily, he landed safely somewhere down the coast. After reflecting on the gravity of the situation, he lost all desire for further attempts. No further operational data on this particular "Bluebird" has been discovered, so its other uses and disposition are not known. The Hess Brothers went on to manufacture the "Argo" biplane and the "Warrior" engine. *(Photo from Stephen J. Hudek Collection.)*

TUXHORN'S BARLING NB-3 - 1929 - LE BLOND 60

Learning to fly — in one day!

Learning to fly an airplane up to solo-flight all in one day's time is still a fair deed and rather unusual; but then, it is nothing new. It has been done on several occasions since this particular time back in 1929. To prove his contention that the average able person could learn to fly quickly and easily, Blaine Tuxhorn, a veteran Kansas City flying-service operator, soloed a 28 year-old truck salesman after eight hours of dual instruction. This was by the way, in the Barling (Nicholas-Beazley) NB-3 low-winged monoplane as shown here. Tuxhorn and Leonard Rhiner, another flight-instructor, took turns of about one hour each to teach young Earl Shaw the basic rudiments of flying the NB-3, all in the same day!

Starting quite early that one fine morning, with only a brief pause for a quick lunch, and then short briefings between each hour, Shaw soloed successfully one time around the patch just as the sun was setting beyond the horizon. The sun finally setting on a very busy, and very eventful day. Inherently stable and quite gentle in its nature, the 65 h.p. LeBlond powered NB-3 helped Shaw considerably, and usually waited patiently while he attempted to sort out his mistakes, and master his air-work. But, it lent no helping hand, you might say, on takeoffs and landings; this really became the hardest part of the all-day session. If you have read, or have heard of someone soloing an airplane after only one day's flight instruction, give him or her their just dues because it is still quite a trick to accomplish. But then, bear in mind too, it has been done before, and it certainly is a helluva lot easier nowadays. *(Photo from Earl C. Reed.)*

DUNN CRUIZAIRE - 1929 - KINNER K5

"Cruizaire" as done by Dunn Manufacturing.

The Dunn "Cruizaire" of 1929, a buxom and waddly-looking three-seater, was little-known outside of its own neighborhood, and that is probably just as well. Offhand, it looks like the designer had good intentions, but wasn't able to make up his mind. That is whether to fashion the airplane something like a scaled-down "Fairchild," or maybe just insert thinly disguised features from many different airplanes. Regardless, it didn't come out looking all that pretty. However, it did have a good wing, carried fuel enough for about five hours of flight (heaven forbid), and the rest of the frame was built good and stout. The engine was the popular five cylinder Kinner K5 of 100 h.p. Being literally bogged-down with all that strength and yet room for three people, the "Cruizaire" was more sedate than spritely! At some 90 m.p.h. at top speed it couldn't be called swifty either.

Its hardy nature kept it around for several years; by 1931 it was reported still flying around somewhere in Kansas. As to its whereabouts after that, we cannot say; it is even possible somebody may find it some day and restore it! Seating two and a pilot, the "Cruizaire" had stiff competition from other ships in its class. It had never been approved by the government in any category. The example shown registered as -616 (serial #1) was quite likely the only one built. Harold L. White, son of "Burt" S. White, assisted in the design and construction of the "Cruizaire." The airplane was originally designed to seat four; the prototype was scaled down to seat three. Incidentally, Burt S. White of Des Moines, Iowa designed and built several of his own airplanes in the light-plane category. "Cruizaire" was manufactured by Dunn Manufacturing Co. of Clarinda, Iowa. Price listed as $4750 at the factory, with standard equipment. *(Photo from Gerald H. Balzer Collection.)*

Elias "Aircoupe" was a convertible.

Elias Brothers of Buffalo, one of the earlier aircraft manufacturers, were great-shakes as plane builders in the early 1920s, but fast-moving progress in aircraft design seemed to have passed them by. Their sporty "Aircoupe" (Model EC-1), one of the first of the coupe-type airplanes, was quite a nifty rig for 1926, but oddly enough it was still being offered as-is as late as 1929. By then, the EC-1 had surely been left behind in the rush to advancement by other light-plane manufacturers, so, people weren't exactly falling over one another to get in line to buy an "Aircoupe!"

Being a "convertible," the snazzy closed-in "coupe" fairing could be left off if one so desired. This, then made it into the drafty "Airsport." It was claimed that the "Sport" was then faster and racier than the "Coupe," but don't you believe it. Either way, that cantankerous six cylinder (two-row radial) Anzani (French) engine of some 80 h.p. had to struggle to its very limit to produce a top speed of 90 m.p.h. It was initially planned to install an 80 h.p. Cato-designed engine, but development of this powerplant was more than Elias Brothers cared to undertake.

Although antiquated for so late in this decade of development, the Elias EC-1 had a strong backbone, simple construction for simple maintenance, and a leisurely attitude. As someone said in comment, if you had a comical outlook in your need for flying, and did not mind being passed up by almost everyone else, this could be the one for you. The EC-1 was never approved by the government in any category, and no reliable tallies were available as to number built. It seems quite probable that only the one example, as shown, was ever built. Designed by Joseph L. Cato, the EX-1 was manufactured by G. Elias & Brothers, Inc. at Buffalo, New York. *(Photo from Gerald H. Balzer Collection.)*

MARCHETTI ARROW - 1930 - MARCHETTI 4 CYL

Marchetti "Arrow" makes its debut.

This was the rare Marchetti "Arrow" designed and built by Marchetti Motor Patents Co. of Oakland, California. The sport-type airplane was apparently a cantilever-winged monoplane of all-wood construction, and powered with a four cylinder air-cooled inline engine of their own design. The incident shown was a test-flight some time in October of 1930. This account is just to show that there was such an airplane as the Marchetti "Arrow." *(Photo from Gerald H. Balzer Collection.)*

BONNEY GULL - 1927 - KIRKHAM 180

The "Bonney Gull" — too much too soon?

The "Bonney Gull" was surely a strange and bizarre attempt in airplane design. Highly streamlined and ahead of its time in some ways, yet awkward and ungainly in others. It plainly was a case of trying to incorporate too many untried features into one machine. Designed by Leonard W. Bonney, who had been flying since 1911, it had been on the drawing-board as a dream for several years. As it finally came out early in 1927, it is perhaps the first time so many advance features were assembled into one airplane. For instance, the bird-like wing was capable of variable incidence, and variable dihedral. There were trailing-edge wing flaps for variable camber, and the wing tips could rotate for lateral balance. For stowage or storing, or towing, the wings could also be folded back! The large faired tail-wheel was steerable, the streamlined landing gear was internally sprung to decrease drag, and the elevators could be adjusted to variable area. We have to bear in mind, all this required yards and yards of complicated linkage, and ingenuous hook-ups which later proved to be too numerous to be practical. To top it off, the cockpit seating two side-by-side was covered with a coupe-top enclosure; it was neatly upholstered and had dual controls.

In reading this description, without actually seeing the real airplane, one might say, "This has got to be one helluva airplane!" Well, on 4 May 1928, the "Gull" was finally rolled out for its moment of truth. And, while many watched, Leonard Bonney was preparing anxiously for his maiden flight in this unusual contrivance. Despite repeated protests from those who knew better, Bonney gunned the 180 h.p. (nine cylinder air-cooled radial) Kirkham engine and off they sped down the runway. The bird-like machine, gathering sufficient speed, lurched off the ground. At about 50 ft. up or so, it wobbled a little, started to fish-tail, and then nosed-over to crash into the ground. Leonard Bonney, who really did believe in his machine, was dead when people reached the scene. It was truly a sad ending for so brave a try. Was the "Bonney Gull" just another man's pipe-dream, or was it just too much too soon? *(Photo from Gerald H. Balzer Collection.)*

CESSNA AS - 1928 - RYAN-SIEMENS SH-12 9 CYL

Siemens-powered Cessna "AS."

If for no other reason, this lovely airplane must be shown because it is such a good likeness of the classic A-series as built by Cessna in the late 1920s. The dainty model "AS," as shown here, powered with the nine cylinder Ryan-Siemens (Siemens-Halske) SH-12 engine of 125 h.p. was quite a delightful combination. Certainly better than the original model "AA" with its 10 cylinder Anzani (French) engine, even though the engine was redesigned by Cessna to be somewhat more reliable. But then, the (German) Siemens-Halske was not always available when ordered, so the engine-airplane combination was not featured by Cessna, unless the buyer could scrounge up his own engine. The modes "AS" was eventually approved on a Group 2 certificate #2-8 (issued 1-5-1929) and all A-series already in service were eligible for this combination when modified to conform. Several of the Cessna A were thus converted, and they were well-liked by those who flew them. *(Photo from Cessna Aircraft Co.)*

Roam-Air "Sport" for Earle Ovington.

Earle Ovington, one of America's "Early Birds," reached a measure of fame by flying the earliest airmail in 1911 on Long Island. Goaded by aviation's skyrocketing success after Charles Lindbergh's trans-Atlantic flight to Paris in 1927, Ovington, like so many others, considered entry into airplane manufacture. He had designed a neat little sport biplane for himself and engaged William J. Waterhouse early in 1929 to engineer it. Development of the airplane ran into several snags because it was originally designed for the five cylinder LeBlond "60" of 65 h.p. and then it was decided to use the seven cylinder LeBlond "90" engine. Finally, the seven cylinder Warner "Scarab" engine of 110 h.p. was selected to give the plane "sport" performance. Later on, an agreement with "Bill" Waterhouse allowed Ovington to use the name "Roamair;" so the little biplane was called the "Roamair Sport." (The name "Roamair" was first used for a Waterhouse-engineered biplane in 1925.)

Like so many other airplanes of 1928-29, Ovington's "Roamair Sport" was offered as a sport-trainer, a plane which could serve the needs of a flight-school operator, or satisfy the whims and fancies of a week-end pilot. As an open cockpit biplane seating two in tandem, it was powered with the popular "Scarab" engine rated 110 h.p. This was considered quite a bit of power back in 1929. The various dimensions and aerodynamic proportions were similar to other planes of this type, and its performance was as good as, or better than most. Of normal construction for the times, the "Sport" was also fully equipped. Some of the features included a metal propeller, wheel brakes, swiveling tail-wheel, adjustable stabilizer, slotted ailerons, upholstered cockpits, and position lights.

Heavier than most airplanes of this type, Ovington's handsome little "Sport" featured strength and lots of good wing area. And capacity, too, for plenty of fuel for the longer cross-country hops. Its price was not listed (you could write in and ask), but believed to be rather high. The "Roamair" by Ovington was never approved for manufacture in any category, and it is quite likely that only the one example was built. It was manufactured by the Roamair Aircraft Corp. of Hollywood, California. *(Photo from Gerald H. Balzer collection.)*

ZENITH Z-6-A -1932 - P&W WASP 420 HP

America's shortest airline.

A. A. Bennett of Bennett Air Transport started his airmail route in the winter of 1932 between Boise and the gold-mining camp at Atlanta, Idaho. This became the shortest contract airmail (C.A.M.) route in the U.S.A. The route was only 65 miles each way, but it was over high treacherous mountains, and there was absolutely no place to land in between. You might say that every winter some 80 families became snow-bound up there, and were practically left stranded from the outside world! The only communication or service they received had to come by air. Or of course, by someone on skis or snow-shoes. It wasn't easy, but Bennett provided these good folks up there with all kinds of services besides bringing their mail. For all this, he used the trusty "Zenith" Z6A cabin biplane as shown here. Powered by the reliable P&W "Wasp" engine of 420 h.p., with ample space for varied cargo, it took more than unusual weather to upset his flight schedules. A tough airplane capable of hard work in primitive areas, the "Zenith" was built in Midway City, California. *(Photo from Peter M. Bowers Collection.)*

SIKORSKY S-39-AL

Operation "Beer Knobs."

The telephone rang impatiently in the operations shack at Roosevelt Field. An excited voice claimed he was the ad-man for Piel Brothers Brewery of Brooklyn, New York. As he was very anxious to get a package aboard the liner "Virginia," he asked if an "amphibian" airplane was available. The only amphibian ready to go at the time was a Sikorsky S-39, so the pilot took the phone for instructions. Briefed quickly on the urgent mission, the pilot pointed out that high winds were making the waters very choppy, and it would be a risky task. But, what the heck, in spite of this, he was willing to take a stab at it!

Relieved and happy, the ad-man arranged for a meeting at Floyd Bennett Airport preferably in the half hour. It seems that New York state, and several other state liquor regulations, required that all bar taps from which beer is drawn be plainly marked by a knob naming the beer being dispensed. Many kegs of "Piels" draft beer had been delivered aboard the liner "Virginia" earlier in the day, but it was not discovered until half hour after she had sailed for Cuba that the required "knobs" had not been put aboard with the kegs. Hence, the urgency of the mission.

Taking off with the package and the ad-man aboard, the S-39 flew on anxiously lest the "Virginia" be well out in the Atlantic Ocean before they got there! Sighting the liner just as a small boat was put over the side, the S-39 swung into position for the delicate job of landing on the swelling sea. As she skimmed above the water, the hull smacked a wave-crest, settled heavily in the trough, and a tip-float buckled under from the force. Riding the swell until the small boat came bobbing alongside, the package was tossed over and taken to the "Virginia." Piel Brothers had lived up to the law and the liner continued its course to Cuba. *(Photo from Sikorsky Aircraft Division.)*

SIMPLEX SPORT CONVER. MONO-BIPLANE - 1929

Simplex "Sport" was convertible.

Simplex Aircraft was not very well known, but they had a talented workforce, and did build some fine airplanes back in the 1920s. Searching for a winner, they developed an unusual "convertible" airplane in 1929, a plane that could be flown usefully as a biplane, or a monoplane. The extra lifting area of the biplane was to allow heavier payloads such as extra fuel for cross-country flying, much more baggage if desired, and there was space enough for small-package cargo. Conversion of the biplane into a sleek monoplane (simply by removing the lower wings) was to provide much greater cruising speeds, and more spirited maneuverability. This was truly to be a sportsman-pilot's airplane!

H. S. "Dick" Myhres brought this airplane to Detroit in 1929 as a part of the annual All-American Aircraft show held at Detroit City Airport. Myhres, being test-pilot and demonstrator for Simplex, was obliged to show it around area airports so that more people could see it; he was tickled to show off the ship's flashy performance. He later flew this airplane as a monoplane in the 1929 National Air Races and entered in five events; sometimes averaging 152 m.p.h. easily around the pylons. Fun-loving Myhres had a ball! All this performance with a stock 225 h.p. Wright J6-7 engine.

As the model R2D (serial #37-R), it was registered as NR-43M; powered with the seven cylinder Wright J6-7-225 engine. It had neither an NACA engine cowl nor a "speed-ring," but these were options for later on. The structure was designed to mount more power if desired. Biplane or monoplane, it was a beautiful machine and many had so remarked. Another frequent remark was something like, "So, who needs it!" The R2D was built only in one example by Simplex Aircraft Corp. at Defiance, Ohio. As model 1W2R when owned by Lou" Tipper of Detroit, its subsequent use or disposition is unknown. *(Photo from Gerald H. Balzer Collection.)*

HEATH SUPER PARASOL SNA-40 - 1931

Heath lands on Chicago Rooftop!

Well, there's nothing unusual about people flocking around to take a peek at the Heath "Super Parasol," because this little nifty attracted attention wherever it went. But, if you'll look closely in upper left-hand corner at the unmistakable retaining wall, you can see that some daring airman landed the Heath on the roof-top of a building! This actually happened in downtown Chicago back in 1931. The daring pilot is the helmeted figure in the upper right-hand corner near the tail-group. Is he perhaps wondering how to get the little bird back home?

As told by "Charlie" Morris, the whole thing was planned as an eye-catching stunt to promote the new "Super Parasol" which Morris had designed. First, a 300 ft. square was marked out on the airport to see how things would go. In practice there were several times the ship would have gone right over the edge, so an arresting gear of sorts was needed as insurance against this. A hand-held length of (bungee) shock-cord did the trick with three husky anchor-men holding onto each side. With the anchor-men in standing position the angle was too high, and the tail always reared up splintering the propeller. Three props later the correct angle was found, and the system seemed to work well enough to try out on the building's rooftop!

Meanwhile, pilot "Duke" Mueller was confident that all would go well — he'd just do it on the rooftop as he had done it many times in the airport square. The ground-crew, however, was slightly bugged by the fact there could be no slip-ups this next time. With newsreel cameras already up in the building, the excitement mounted. High over Chicago, Mueller lined up carefully on the 300 ft. square on the rooftop — geez, it looked so damned small!! Well, here goes, oops, golly we made it! A volley of cheers went up and then a sigh of relief by everyone, perhaps even Mueller. For the take-off back to the airport, a wooden ramp had been built up over the parapet. "Duke" gunned the engine for all it was worth and got off the roof in fine shape, playfully bouncing his wheels on the ramp as he soared off the building.

The whole Heath clan was extremely happy it went off so well, but I suppose to one like "Duke" Mueller, it was just another outing. The whole incident, including the landing and then the take-off, was on movie-film, but the cameras purposely failed to reveal the "arresting gear" or the wooden ramp built over the parapet. It must have looked quite exciting on the movie-screen. The airplane was a Heath SNA-40 which was an LNA-40 with clipped wings! *(Photo from Gerald H. Balzer Collection.)*

AVRO AVIAN 594 - CIRRUS III

Lady Mary Heath.

Lady Mary Heath, famous British aviatrix, was a good pilot and all spunk. Hoisting a well-turned leg up into the cockpit of an airplane was typical of her character and her will. Nevertheless, she was quite a lady. The airplane shown was an Avro "Avian," a British lightplane the lady used to promote the new American Cirrus Engines around the countryside of America. The modest young fellow who politely looks away while the Lady bares a "neat gam" was "Lew" Reisner of Kreider-Reisner. If the lady hadn't been proud of her shapely legs, she would have surely worn britches! *(Photo from Fairchild-Hiller Corp.)*

CURTISS-BLEECKER - 1930 - PRATT & WHITNEY WASP 9 CYL

Curtiss-Bleecker helicopter.

Imagine someone inventing a hilarious contraptions such as is shown here (it's supposed to be a helicopter) and then actually smile about it! This, then, was the hush-hush Curtiss-Bleecker "helicopter," a machine of such whimsy and complexity that it is almost impossible to describe. Let alone, tell how it was supposed to work! (Please don't ask.)

Needless to say, an awful lot of time and good money was expended on this project just to see it bounce up and down a few times, and then just literally come apart at every joint (and, gads there were so many), and then lay there smoking in a pile of very expensive junk! Why they had two seats in the thing is a puzzle indeed — who would be brave enough to go along, anyhow? It is painful to think, without flinching too, that there could have been an earlier version of this contraption because -373N as shown was listed as serial #2.

The photo was taken 6-18-30 with a nine cylinder Pratt and Whitney "Wasp" engine installed. (It apparently took that much power just to twirl all of those parts around.) Levity aside, M. B. Bleecker, the project engineer on the machine's development, really did believe the concept would work! But, sadly enough for Bleecker and for Curtiss-Wright, it did not. *(Photo from H. Lloyd Child Collection.)*

GRANVILLE BOTHERS ASCENDER - AERONCA E-107-A 28 HP

This is a "Gee Bee????"

Granville Brothers had made their mark in aviation by building racing airplanes. As the "Gee Bee" line they will be forever remembered as the fastest, the meanest, and most controversial airplanes of the "Golden Age" of air-racing history. Just to be doing something between air-racing seasons, the brothers honed and refined their airplanes for the next season. Or, sometimes they all got together on some fun project to take their minds off the pressing problems. One of these projects, as is shown here, was certainly not what one would expect coming from the "Gee Bee" shop. Most likely fashioned for laughs, the ship was a comical-looking "canard-type" that reportedly was built in a week or so. Some one with a definite sense of humor named it the "Ascender," knowing full well that this would soon be translated into "Ass-Ender!!"

Built around an "Aeronca" wing, the odd-looking ship was nothing but a bunch of welded steel tubing hurriedly fashioned into shape and structure to fit the purpose. This was then covered mostly in fabric. A well-used two cylinder Aeronca E-107-A engine of 28 h.p. provided the means of thrust and motivation. The gang had fun with it for a while, but brother Mark smashed it up on one of its hops. It was eventually relegated to the scrap heap. The "Ascender" was registered as X-757N as serial #Q-1. It certainly didn't look it, but it really was a genuine "Gee Bee!" *(A Frederic Ruther photo.)*

K-R "Challenger" mounts a "Ranger" V-12.

The popular Kreider-Reisner "Challenger" biplane was of particularly robust airframe, and when it came into the family of "Fairchild" airplanes as the KR-series, it served often as a test-bed for various aircraft engines. When Fairchild was perfecting their model 6-390 (six cylinder air-cooled inverted inline) engine, it was installed in a "K-R" biplane for test, development and certification. When the line of engines known as the "Ranger" was broadened to include a 12 cylinder air-cooled, inverted vee-type engine, it was also flight-tested in a K-R "Challenger" biplane as shown here.

This airplane-engine combination was designated the Model 140, and the engine, later to be known as the "Ranger," was the model V-770, rated 240-300 h.p. It is quite likely this engine turned the "K-R" biplane into a feisty airplane with all this extra power. It could have been offered as a high-performance "Sport" for the sportsman-pilot. But, when the testing was over, the engine was pulled out and the airplane brought back to standard KR-34-C specifications. As shown, X-756Y was serial #S-801 registered to the American Airplane and Engine Corp. They had, for a time, taken over some of Fairchild's activities during the early depression of the 1930s. *(Photo from Fairchild-Hiller Corp.)*

Hawke "Duster" wages war on California bugs.

Crop-dusting, crop-spraying, and seeding by airplane has been important to agriculture for many, many years. In more recent years it has grown to be a big business, and there are several airplanes on the market that were especially designed for this kind of work. But, let's say, 50-60 years ago, it was quite unusual to see an airplane especially designed just for that purpose. Most "dusters" and "sprayers" (since 1925) were of necessity just modifications of aircraft that were acceptable for the job because of their performance, capacity, or easy-enough conversion.

The "Salinas Valley" in California had always depended on the crop-duster quite heavily, and everyday problems in this food-growing area had developed special equipment and techniques to suit the job. Surely, that's why the Hawke "Duster" was developed, and certain operating criteria dictated its design. For more positive visibility in critical areas, the pilot sat up front, or upstream of his load of chemical dust or spray. This then suggested, more or less, the high-wing monoplane configuration which worked out quite well in service. It is fair to say that no flying-job in aviation can be as taxing, nor as demanding as being a good "duster-pilot." The working duster-pilot spends most of his time while in the air "on the deck" while dodging trees, poles, and wires, yet ensuring a proper coverage without excessive overlap. Years ago, during a particularly heavy season, one over-worked duster-pilot jokingly complained he spent so much time just barely off the ground that he was getting nervous when above 200 ft.!

The Hawke "Duster" as shown here, was powered with the Wright "Whirlwind" J5 engine of 220 h.p. Under arrangement, it usually operated with an experimental or restricted license. According to record, it was designed and built entirely by the Hawke people for their own use. Three airplanes were built. NX-10609 was ship #1, NR-10626 was ship #2, and NR-10627 was ship #3; all were registered (1930-31) to E. R. Hawke of Modesto, California where most of the operating was performed by "Hawke Dusters." *(Photo from Gerald H. Balzer Collection.)*

ROBERTSON WATER-PLANE - 1930

The Robertson "Water-Plane."

Man has always used imagination to give himself a thrilling ride, better yet if it was dangerous. Short of actual flying, there have been all sorts of ice-sleds pushed around a frozen lake by an engine-driven propeller. Or, flat-bottomed air-boats driven usually by an airplane engine with a shrouded pusher-propeller for skimming along in marshy swamps. But, this contraption pictured here is one that surely has not been tried very often. It beats one to understand the purpose of it, but a ride is a ride! Even if (or especially if) it's unique and only draws attention. Built and operated in 1930, this machine was called the Robertson "Water-Plane" — the locale of the incident shown is not known. The miserable depression-days of the 1930s prompted restless souls to contrive all sorts of diversions! Reflecting on it, one wonders if a good yank on "the stick" would tend to create the top half of an inside loop, and a thorough dunking, not to mention the surprise! *(Photo from Gerald H. Balzer Collection.)*

MIAMI MAID MM-1 - 1929 - MENASCO-SALMSON 230 HP

"Miami Maid" finds a home in Buzzard's Bay.

The "Miami Maid" MM-1 has been described as a hurriedly put-together hybrid consisting of a modified Curtiss F (wooden) flying-boat hull to which was fastened a modified "Fokker" wing (probably from a "Universal"). The original power for this craft was a nine cylinder Menasco-Salmson air-cooled radial engine of 230 h.p. (as shown here at Miami) mounted high atop the cantilever wing in a "pusher" position. With room for four in a gaping open cockpit forward, a tip-float under each wing, and a multitude of other drag-producing features, the "Maid" had comparatively poor performance. When loaded, it required nearly full power at all times to fly at all! The cockpit was later enclosed with a cabin of sorts, the engine mounting was enclosed in a nacelle, but all that wasn't really much help. The installation of a nine cylinder Wright R-975 (J-6 series) engine of 300 h.p. was of some help, but still the overall performance was far from exhilarating.

Duly researched it had not been determined who designed, or who built the "Miami Maid," nor where the money came from to build it. The manufacturer was the Miami Aircraft Corp. of Miami, Florida. Oddly enough, the airplane was approved on a Group 2 certificate #2-173 issued 1-11-30. It has been reported that an aviation-minded millionaire named Col. "Ned" Green of South Darmouth, Massachusetts had offered to buy the "Maid" provided it was delivered to his estate. Ed Nirmaier, the company demo-pilot came with the deal. The flying-boat was apparently bought for Mrs. Green's use — Mr. Green did not care to fly. The well-to-do Green family's imposing estate was on Buzzard's Bay from where the "Maid" was occasionally flown. No further operational data, nor final disposition was available. *(R. B. Hoit Photo.)*

STUDENT PRINCE - 1929

Briefly — the "Student Prince" danced at the "Ball."

This nifty little two-seater looks like it could stand-up with the best of them in its class despite its humble beginning. The prototype of this design was actually the second airplane built by students and staff at the Adcox Aviation trade School in Portland, Oregon. To keep the students busy in the learning of aircraft manufacture, it was a project designed for the requirements of a Portland-area pilot who had financed the project. Because the state of Oregon was lax in upholding federal regulations, which were stiff and extensive, the airplane would only be allowed to fly within the confines of the state. This seemed to be a suitable arrangement for all concerned. Designed by Basil Smith, who it appears had some knowledge and a good eye for airplanes, the newly designed airplane first appeared as the Adcox SP, -263V as serial #101.

The project was started in the Fall of 1929, and the airplane was delivered in the Spring of 1930, right into the teeth of the growing depression! Designed initially as a sport-trainer, it was rolled out for all to see as a rather handsome-looking machine with a pleasing aerodynamic form. Repeated tests proved excellent flight characteristics, and it seemed to have a nature and behavior that was a happy-medium for a trainer. All in all, it seemed also to have the recipe that would instill the pride of ownership. Its stance and behavior attracted the likes of "Tex" Rankin, and a few other notables with money in hand, who got together and formed Aircraft Builders, Inc.

The new firm had a plant just outside of Portland. With a work-force of five or so, the eager bunch started on a batch of six airplanes. Very few changes were made from the original design, and the production model was christened the "Student Prince." Cautiously and rightfully so, it was presented for a Group 2 approval, receiving #2-258 issued on 8-14-30. Oddly enough, the approval was awarded for three airplanes only (#101-102-103). If the total of six were built as proposed, it seems that at the outset some of the "Student Princes" were restricted to operating in Oregon only.

The approved airplane was powered with the A.C.E. Cirrus Mk. 3 of 90 h.p. rated. It compared well with other airplanes of this type, and fared well in general with its pleasant nature. The "Cirrus Mk. 3" was a continuous headache to pilots who expected better reliability, so it was not unusual nor uncommon to see the "Prince" decked out with a more reliable radial engine on its nose. Some were seen about with the five cylinder Kinner K5 of 100 h.p., the Warner "Scarab" of 110 h.p., and one was reported with the seven cylinder "Comet" engine. Whether that be so or not, there was one actually seen in later years at a popular fly-in with a "Continental" 220 hung on its nose! Now there's one that must have been a real barn-burner! Because of extensive modifications to this design in later years, it was finally classed as amateur-built. *(Photos from Gerald H. Balzer Collection.)*

The "Student Prince" poses another view.

AMERICAN EAGLE A-1 - 1927-28 - SALMSON 120 HP

"American Eagle" with (French) Salmson engine.

Outside of being a super-neat photo of a 1928 "American Eagle" A-1 biplane, the only thing outstanding about this airplane, to any extent, is the engine. This installation was the nine cylinder (French) Salmson engine of 120 h.p. A pretty fair engine, but its availability was unpredictable and spare parts were hard to come by. So, this was one of only perhaps a few examples in this combination. A little-known fact is that the stalwart "American Eagle" biplane of 1927-28 was available or at least tested with just about anything that would turn a propeller! There were such as the 10 cylinder (French) Anzani, the six cylinder inline (U.S.A.) Aeromarine, the Quick radial (a Rhone rotary converted to static radial), the eight cylinder vee-type (French) Hispano-Suiza, and of course, the (German) Siemens-Halske. All of these installations had their particular merit; in most cases the buyer of an "Eagle" would send his own engine, whatever it may be, to the factory for installation and they did get some doozies! Except for the Siemens-Halske and the Hispano-Suiza installation, none of these other combinations were ever approved. *(Photo from Gerald H. Balzer Collection.)*

Johnnie Dull, a young Eskimo lad who had never seen a movie, used a telephone, driven an automobile, nor rode in an elevator, came down to visit Seattle in 1935. Fascinated by airplanes he decided to learn to fly. Though it may sound incredible, he actually set some sort of local record by "soloing" after only 90 minutes of dual instruction! Proving without doubt that Johnnie Dull was not so dull, after all. It was really no harder than operating a "Kayak" in a swift Alaskan stream.

Up and away on a full head of steam!

On 12 April 1933, a well-used "Travel Air" biplane made history on the first-ever flight of a steam-driven airplane carrying a man. William J. Besler had made three successful flights that morning from the Municipal Airport in Oakland, California and pronounced the tests as very satisfactory. Up to this time all successful steam-powered flights were made with airplane models, notably by Stringfellow and Langley, but not carrying a man. Designed by George D. and William J. Besler, the first practical, external combustion power-plant for an airplane was a two cylinder double-acting engine in a 90 degree "vee." Altogether, it did weigh just a little more than the Curtiss OX-5 engine that was originally in the airplane.

The Besler steam-engine was test-run on a stand for some 30 hours before being put in the airplane, and then for 20 hours more of ground-testing after being installed in the "Travel Air." All tests went reasonably well, so it was decided to make the flight on the day of 12 April. Excited by the history-making event, observers remarked about the unusual quiet of the engine and its seemingly effortless power. Using 90% of the power, only the rumble of the fire, which was burning furnace oil, could be heard above the propeller noise.

It was noticed, too, that take-offs were shorter, climb-out was strong, and landing was relatively shorter because the "prop" could be put into reverse just after touch-down. In all, it was a very impressive accomplishment, and the Besler Brothers promised several improvements on their next steam-engine especially designed for airplanes. They stated, however, that the potential for a satisfactory steam power-plant was not nearly so good in the lower power outputs as there would be, in say, the 1000 h.p. range or higher. The Beslers were convinced that the external combustion engine, namely a steam-engine, showed great promise for powering the larger airliners. A capital idea, no less, but somewhere along the way the idea and its potential ran out of steam. *(Photo from Gerald H. Balzer Collection.)*

AUTOGIRO COMPANY PITCAIRN - 1933 - POBJOY 75-90

James Ray taxis part of the way home!

James Ray, flying an experimental Pitcairn "autogiro" was returning home from the National Air Races for 1935 held at Cleveland, Ohio. He had taken off in weather which had proved impenetrable to other pilots. But, because of an extremely lower ceiling in the mountains, he finally had to land by the roadside at Blandburg, Pa. With his rotor blades first folded back, he then taxied the autogiro, which was designed to be more or less roadable, up the highway for about 10 miles to reach Tyrone. Now safely beyond the highest ridges of the Alleghenies, he drove into a small roadside field; here he unfolded the rotor blades and took off for home.

By following the Juniata Valley out of the mountains, he completed his trip to Philadelphia. The small autogiro he was flying was a prototype built for the Bureau of Air Commerce to test the concept. The machine had been on display at the Air Races and had stirred up much interest in its capabilities. A truly roadable version built later had axle-drive to its road wheels for better handling. With its rotor blades folded back, it was about the size of a smaller automobile. Many ideas for a "roadable" have been tried over the years, but none reached the goal intended. *(Photo from Emil Strasser.)*

Testing the Kimball "Beetle."

The development of new engines for aircraft in the 1928-29 period was about as frantic as the development of new airplanes. Among the crop of engines then available were several that went on to become basic power-plants for some of our best airplanes. But, some of these engines offered in the haste were not particularly note-worthy, and some were even fairly crude in design and assembly. Shown here on a test-stand in Hagerstown, Maryland is the seven cylinder Kimball "Beetle" as tested by the Kreider-Reisner Division of Fairchild for possible use in their popular KR-34 line of biplanes. The tests apparently had not been altogether satisfactory, so the "Beetle" was not considered favorably for use in their production airplanes.

The Kimball "Beetle" was a seven cylinder air-cooled, radial-type engine of normal configuration and make-up, except for its cylinder head and valve-gear design. The "intake" was a side-valve built into the cylinder barrel, and the "exhaust"was a valve-in-head operated by a push-rod. The sequence of each valve was operated by a cam disc. This was generally known as the "F-Head" type which actually was of no particular advantage in an aircraft engine. The "Beetle" was a rather big engine displacing 585 cu. in., and at 380 lbs. dry, less hub and starter, was fairly heavy per horsepower. Rated 135 h.p. at 1800 r.p.m., the engine was to sell for $2900 crated at the factory. Manufactured by Kimball Aircraft Corp. of Naugatuck, Connecticut, the Kimball people apparently loaned out a few engines for test in various airplanes, but none achieved any particular success. A KR-32 (serial #148) with the 135 h.p. Kimball "Beetle" was registered as -5015 to Kimball Aircraft for test and development. *(Photo from Fairchild-Hiller Corp.)*

STARWING G-4 - 1928 - LE BLOND 60

Phil Goembel builds a "Starwing."

The saucy little low-winger pictured here was the "Starwing" model G-4, a design by Phil Goembel, an old-timer from Massillon, Ohio. After a period of time used up for design and construction, the airplane was christened in a local ceremony on 22 July 1928. The mayor of the town officiated and was honored as the very first passenger. Being a jack-of-all-trades, Goembel was president, chief engineer, sales manager, and holder of 52% of the stock in the newly formed Starwing Corp. As a shake-down for the perky little airplane, Goembel used the "Starwing" often to barnstorm the countryside of Ohio during the summer season. In a way, this helped to support his manufacturing operation

while waiting for someone to order one of his airplanes. The "Starwing" was a good little airplane, but it must be said, competition in the airplane-building business for this type of airplane was rather fierce during this time, especially in Ohio!

The "Starwing" seated two in tandem out in the airy open, and was powered with the five cylinder (Ohio-built) LeBlond "60" engine. Just from the looks of its proportions, it probably was a fun ship to fly if you paid attention. And, it looks rugged enough to go just about anywhere, which it usually did. Construction of the wing and fuselage framework was quite typical for the times — more or less Plain-Jane, and no innovations. You might say its only outstanding features were its thick, strut-braced wing and its wide-tread landing gear. The ship numbered X-5529 (as shown) was the prototype of the "Starwing" series, and it is believed that there was another example built of this same model. The "Starwing" G-4 was never approved in any category, but Goembel was planning to get an approval. The G-4 was manufactured by the Starwing Corp., but it was also registered to the American Aircraft Co. of Massillon, Ohio. Final disposition of the airplane is not known. *(Photo from Gerald H. Balzer Collection.)*

WARREN CP-1 - 1928 - COMET 130

The Warren CP-1

Pictured here is a simple, three-place high-winged monoplane built for H. G. Warren in 1929 at California Poly-Tech as an exercise for the students of aeronautics at the college. Registered as the Warren CP-1 (X-501M was serial #1). It was powered with a seven cylinder "Comet" 7-D engine of 130 h.p. The design and construction was very basic for the time, and not even old-time learned hangar-fliers know very much about this one. *(Photo from Gerald H. Balzer Collection).*

FOKKER TRI-MOTOR F-7A-3M - 1927

Hitch-hike to Washington, D.C. — fly back.

This account was an adventure that is not likely to happen in this day and age, but it did happen back in early 1927. Two young newspaper women, Doris Day and Anita Grannis, were anxious to know what it would be like to fly in one of those new talked-about Fokker "Tri-Motor" (F7-3M) airliners. As shown here, it was the Flag-Ship of the Philadelphia Rapid Transit Line on a route from Philadelphia to Washington, D.C. and back.

For several weeks the young ladies skimped and saved up their money for a one-way fare, plus a little more for walking-around-money. Then, they hitch-hiked the 125 miles from Philadelphia to the Nation's capitol. It took them about 19 $^{1}/_{2}$ hours. Boarding the huge airplane for the trip was a real thrill for them, and the flight back to "Philly" was a 1 $^{1}/_{2}$ hour ride they would remember for a long, long time! When asked upon their return, both of the young ladies vowed it was all well worth it, and looked forward to doing it again. Only next time they would save up enough money to fly both ways! *(A U.S. Air Force Photo.)*

In 1936, Yankee (American) mercenary-pilots were flying and fighting on both sides of the fracas during the Spanish Civil War. Both warring sides, trying to lure good pilots from one another, were offering $1500 per month as base pay with a chance to earn bonuses. They were paying $2500 per month for a pilot with an airplane. Many pilots left for Spain and so did a lot of good airplanes.

HOCKADAY COMET - 1937

Noel Hockaday builds a "Comet."

Noel Hockaday was well known in the aircraft-manufacturing business. He designed and helped build plenty of good little airplanes for other people. In 1937, he decided to design and build an airplane for himself. This, then, as shown here was the sporty-looking Hockaday "Comet" (first called the "Noelcraft"), a nifty two-seated sport monoplane eager to take a stance among those of its kind. As the "Comet" it made its formal debut for all to see in South California. Flitting around the state in a show-off mood, it waited a time for acceptance, but had to sneak offstage never to return. It's a pity, too, because the ship did have appeal and some potential too. Manufactured by the Hockaday Aircraft Corp. of Burbank, California, Noel R. Hockaday was president and general manager and W. H. Yarick was vice president and chief engineer. *(Photo from Robert S. Hirsch Collection.)*

This is your Captain Speaking!

This photograph should make one realize just how far we have come in some 60-odd years of aviation progress. The amazement is not so much in aircraft development, although the strides have been great to be sure, but mostly in the development of what is now reverently called the Pilot-Captain — the man in charge. Hence, we look at the pilot-captain shown here as he's about to take off on a flight to somewhere in Ohio. This scene surely emphasizes the difference in attitude of pilot-captains that has developed over the years. Back then, in more innocent times, a twist of the billed cap to the rear and he is ready to be off to his destination. Upon arriving, the cap is turned around again to the front. A moment or two later, even in the airport-restaurant, no one would ever guess he had just flown in with a load of passengers from Cincy, Toledo, Cleveland, or wherever. A far cry we should say from the natty uniformed pilot-captain of more recent years. Nowadays, he struts by in his impeccable dress, toting a bulging brief-case filled with heaven knows what, a co-pilot to do most of his flying, and a covey of lovely stewardesses that practically curtsy as his eminence walks by. Yessir, in watching the scene unfold for lo' these many years 'tis hard to realize just how far we have come since then!

The "airliner" shown here is the International F-18 of 1928-29 vintage, the particular pride of one Edwin Fisk who designed it. Built up largely of wood, plywood veneer, bits of steel, and yards and yards of airplane-grade cloth. All of this muffled noise in the passenger's cabin, and ironed out vibrations from the engine. 'Twas said, the docile F-18 was matronly, very friendly, and practically flew itself. One pilot had jokingly asked to have put in extra padding and arm rests in his cockpit so he could enjoy his leisure in more comfort. The cabin forward seated four or five in plush mohair comfort, while the pilot-captain was seated in an open cockpit aft where he wouldn't be disturbed. The pilot actually had a seat to his right, but this was not for a co-pilot. It was generally reserved for the sporty-type passenger who paid extra for this seat. This passenger would be the one that would rather sit back there to relish the elements, and watch the pilot fly the plane, rather than be cooped up in the stuffy ol' cabin.

Usually powered with the nine cylinder Wright "Whirlywind" J5C engine of 220 h.p., the F-18 cruised about 100 m.p.h., if the wind was right, and its overall ability was such that any little dirt-strip just outside of town was ample for a base of operations. Born and reared in Long Beach, California, some F-18 type were also built in Ancor, Ohio, and the move to Jackson, Michigan saw the end of the line. Yessir, we have come a long way since then — one often pauses to wonder if we haven't come too far!!! *(A Winstead Brothers Photo.)*

INTERNATIONAL F-18 - 1928-29 - WRIGHT WHIRLWIND J5C

International F-18 "airliner" serviced by a crew of one!

AKERMAN JDA-8 FLIVVER - 1931 - SZELEKLY 45 HP

Professor Akerman builds a "Flivver."

Professor John D. Akerman, teaching at the University of Minnesota, was an engineering consultant sought out by many airplane designers and manufacturers of this period. They say he had quite a knack for solving aeronautical problems, and suggesting design criteria to improve utility, speed, and performance. Solving the vexing problems of others was a challenge he enjoyed; but, in 1930-31 he was bitten by the "flivver-plane" bug. For two years, he toyed with several concepts that showed promise. Feeling that the normal configuration for an airplane was not entirely suitable for a low-powered airplane used for sport, Akerman fashioned more suitable ideas into a flivver-plane that was suitable, but far from normal.

The Akerman JDA-8, as shown, was a high-winged monoplane with a pusher-type (Szekely 45 h.p.) engine installation. The tail-group was out on a triangular-truss boom which also protected people from walking into the propeller arc. The pod-type fuselage was slung low on a three-wheeled landing gear making access to the cockpit very easy. The open cockpit seated two side-by-side (though snugly) and its placement in front of everything offered the maximum in visibility. Built and put together in a shop on the Wold-Chamberlain airport, the JDA-8 was rolled out with some local fanfare in March of 1931. The Northland Aviation Co. was formed, but production was never realized. X-897K was serial #1 which later had Jacobs 3-55 engine registered to John D. Akerman. The JDA-8 was to sell for less than $1000. *(Photo from Gerald H. Balzer Collection.)*

HANDLEY-PAGE 0-400 AIR EXPRESS - 1919 - V-1500

Air Express to Chicago . . . almost!

The busy-looking scene pictured was really an occasion of historical significance. It was the first experiment with full-scale air-express shipments. Much like the old-fashioned "bucket brigade," a truck-load of air-express packages are being loaded into the belly of a four-engined (British) Handley-Page V-1500 converted World War I bomber. Being loaded here by employees of the American Railway Express Co., the eager line seems to include everyone from the errand-boy up to the president (that must be he on the right looking on). This was the morning of 14 November 1919 on Mitchell Field in Long Island, New York. The huge four-engined biplane was scheduled to fly non-stop to Chicago to demonstrate the time saving possible with deliveries of shipments by air-express.

Winging its way finally toward Chicago in majestic grandeur, stiff headwinds (some built in?) and some pesky engine troubles forced the converted cargo-plane to land reluctantly on a rough bit of field in Mt. Jewett, Pennsylvania. The packages were then quickly transferred by truck to the next Chicago-bound train. Thus by accident, establishing the first express shipments to travel in combined air-rail service. After this experiment, many others were tried, of course, (the Handley-Page was dismantled and sent back to England) and before long shipments of air-express were criss-crossing the nation almost on a daily basis. Today, thousands of communities located off the airline routes enjoy air-express service through the coordination of air and rail facilities. Shipments nowadays will arrive quickly and safely, but probably not be handled with the enthusiasm and earnest hustle that is shown here above. *(Photo from Joseph P. Juptner Collection.)*

CYCLOPLANE GROUND TRAINER - 1930

Learning to fly without leaving the ground!

Back in 1930, they devised this little winged go-cart to entice more people into learning how to fly. Oddly enough, many people still suffered in the thoughts of being severed from good ol' earth and taken abruptly to some great height. Then being told, here take the stick, and see how easy it is to fly! Well, the chattering feet on the rudder pedals, and the sweaty grip on the stick, would usually produce a pattern of flight sure to convince the reluctant student that this flying business was meant for a special kind of man, and surely not he! This he suspected all along.

CYCLOPLANE 2-SEAT - 1931 - CYCLOMOTOR

Two-seated Trainer

To eliminate the dormant fear in people's minds, those that felt more secure with their feet on the ground (rather than being hung precariously from about 30 ft of wing), the ground-trainer was developed. This was a machine largely resembling a flying-machine, to teach the apprehensive student the mechanics of piloting an airplane. That is, without the burden of fear that he would fall to the ground if they made a mistake, and with control enough to raise or lower the nose, to bank the wings, and to execute turns without leaving the ground. As shown on the previous page, it looks like it might have been harmless fun. The pilot need hardly fear of getting hurt, unless he ran into a tree, or something.

This one would really fly!

O. L. Woodson, a reputable airplane designer, and H. S. "Dick" Myhres, a cracker-jack pilot, for want of something to do, revived the idea of the "Penguin" ground-trainer, one similar to that used in some pilot-training schools in the early part of World War I. Woodson and Myhres devised a method of training that actually required three different machines. The student was taken out first for a few short hops in a dual control ground-trainer; then allowed to solo for a time in the single-seater as shown. When fears subsided and fairly good knowledge was demonstrated as to what all the controls were for, and what they did when he wiggled and waggled them, the student was about ready for a solo-hop in the powered "Cycloplane." The Cycloplane was a real-airplane version of the two previous machines. A network of these schools had been planned for installation all over the country, but apparently it wasn't such a good idea after all. Those that actually wanted to learn to fly went to regular flying-schools anyhow. *(Photos from Gerald H. Balzer Collection.)*

BUTLER SKYWAY (CHANGED TO BLACKHAWK)

The case of the missing "Blackhawk!"

In trying to track down the identity (registration number) of Butler "Blackhawk" #2 (serial #101) for a chapter in *U. S. Civil Aircraft, Volume 2,* we came upon the story of Wilton Briney, a fellow later known around Kansas City as ol' fumble-fingers! Wilton Briney, as Butler Aircraft's test-pilot, went up to test ship #1 (serial #100) in the morning and busted it up somewhat on landing. Anxious to see at least one of their airplanes make a good showing, the crew rolled out ship #2 (serial #101) for its maiden hop. Everything went well until our Hero, Wilton Briney, came in to land and smashed this one to pieces also! It was damaged so badly that they removed the engine, and a few other odd pieces they could salvage.

So, the crux of the matter is that ship #2 (serial #101) was demolished as a brand-new airplane before it could receive its registration number from the Aeronautics Branch of the Department of Commerce. Therefore, statistic buffs and historians take note, the #2 "Blackhawk" (serial #101) will not appear on any registration listings. As to what happened to Wilton Briney — he was asked to find employment elsewhere. The airplane shown here is ship #1 (serial #100) as it later took on a useful career with a large contracting firm. *(Photo from Smithsonian National Air Museum.)*

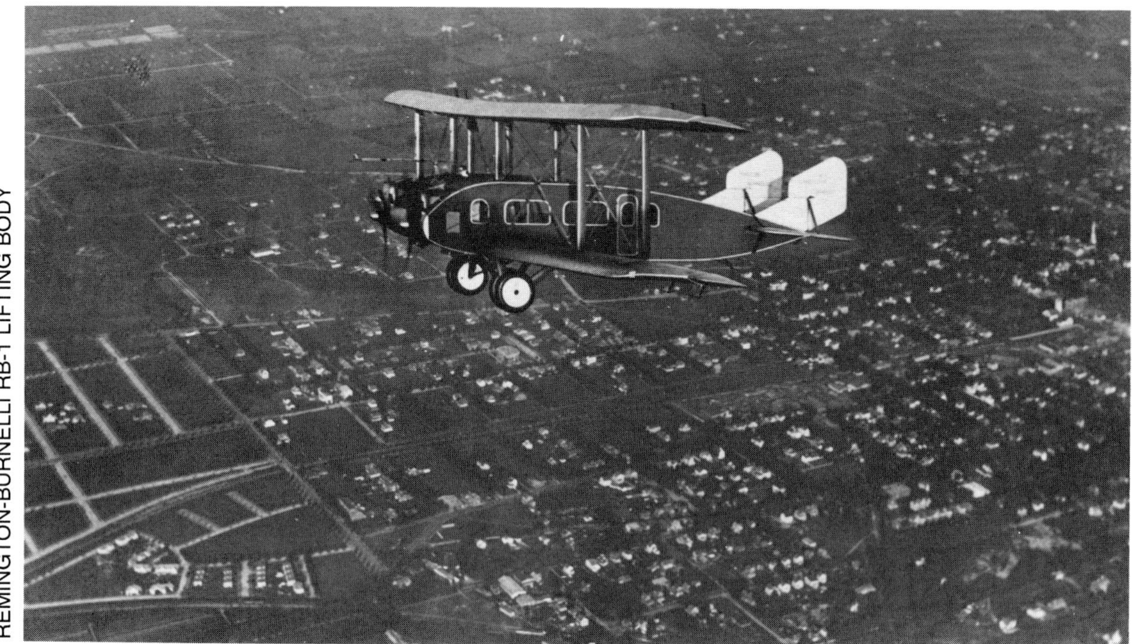
REMINGTON-BURNELLI RB-1 LIFTING BODY

The first "lifting-body" airplane.

There has been discussion now and then about who was the first to design the "lifting-body" airplane. General consensus seems to be lately (among those too young to know any better) that it was NASA that developed the idea. Actually, it was Vincent J. Burnelli, a pioneer in aviation for over 50 years, who originated the idea in 1920. At that time he applied for a patent, a patent that was finally granted in May of 1930. The huge Remington-Burnelli RB-1 (as shown over Keyport, New Jersey) was the first successful lifting-body airplane; it provided ample room in its massive body for 25 passengers and two pilots. The "airfoiled" fuselage, of course, contributed greatly to the overall lift. Spanning some 74 ft., the big biplane was powered with two 12 cylinder vee-type "Liberty" engines of 425 h.p. each.

Plagued with some minor control problems, the RB-1 crashed and was partially demolished in mid-1923. After some redesign, an RB-2 was built with two "Galloway" engines, and it first flew in 1924. On one flight, after becoming lost in a heavy fog, it ran out of fuel and landed in an offshore swamp suffering damage. The RB-2 with its huge area inside the "air-foiled body" was designed to haul air-cargo, and became well-known nationwide as a "flying showroom" by hauling an "Essex" sedan (inside the cabin) all around the country. This was to prove the airplane, and promote sales for the automobile. At one time in its existence, the RB-2 was also powered with two (British) Rolls-Royce "Condor" engines.

The model CB-3 of 1929 was a twin-engined, high wing monoplane powered with two 12 cylinder Curtiss "Conqueror" engines of 600 h.p. each. It was also seen all around the country, and deemed quite successful. All of the

Burnelli "lifting-body" designs after that had been monoplanes. The Burnelli designs had all flown satisfactorily, carried great loads, and had proven his concept ably, but the idea as such was never accepted. The old RB-2 and subsequent airplanes, after being stored idly, were eventually cut up for scrap! The CBY-3 "Loadmaster" built in Canada (1945-47) was his last example of the lifting-body type. In 1968, the CBY-3 was offered to several museums — it may still be around somewhere as an example of Vincent Burnelli's dream to make that break-through in the science of aerodynamics. In the meantime, the lifting-body designs by NASA (National Aerospace Administration) were a highly sophisticated approach to the same idea, but they in no way resembled the designs of Burnelli! *(Photo from Charles W. Meyers Collection.)*

NICHOLSON JUNIOR KN-1 - 1930

The Nicholson "Junior."

This aerial go-cart was the Nicholson "Junior" KN-1. As the pride and joy of H. G. Nicholson, Jr. of New York, it was a single-place, open monoplane powered with a three cylinder Szekely SR-3L engine of 35 h.p. Shown here on 13 December 1930, it stands as a shoulder-wing strut-braced monoplane designed for low-cost sport flying. X-799V was serial #1, and it is quite likely that this was the only example built. In fairness, one could say it is a cute airplane, but its utility and reason for being would be highly personal and very limited. A KN-2 with swept-back folding wings, with side-by-side seating for two, was also proposed with a Continental A-40 engine. *(Photo from Charles W. Meyers Collection.)*

A notice in a 1930s periodical. We are happy to report that Allen H. Nightingale finally soloed the "Swallow" at Eagle Airport. His instructor was Harvey Crow!

HOPKINS-MEADE SPORTPLANE - 1927

San Diego home-built.

Those that have been around airplanes for any time, know the home-built airplane movement is certainly not new. They have been doing it since the Wright Brothers heaved one into space back in 1903! After the lull of World War I, there was a strong revival of the movement in the early 1920s, and another good surge of enthusiasm for the home-built putt-putt again during the 1930s. This was a time when the great "depression" was about at its lowest ebb, and the flying-folk had to do something.

A home-built airplane is definitely a mark of self-expression. One often wonders what the heck that guy was thinking of when you see some of the contraptions that were built in past years. Although we hasten to concede that some very fine home-builts have graced these rutted ol' skies, and very often some aeronautical first had quietly been uncovered. Often, something that even astounded the learned aeronautical engineers!

You are wondering when comes the punch-line to this little ditty; well, there is none, really. It just came to mind one might like to see this little home-built pictured here, and get a chuckle or two. The vee-bottom fuselage you will notice, was an excellent way to achieve streamlining and lower airframe weight. But, they must have missed the fact that it provided no room for rudder pedals, nor the pilot's big feet! Well heck, that was not such a problem after all it seems. Two foot-holes provided the necessary room, and anyway, a sport-plane was supposed to be breezy.

Shown here at San Diego, California, this little charger was built early in 1927 by W. F. Hopkins and T. Meade who apparently had been around air-planes a bit because the little "parasol" monoplane shows evidence of good design ideas. the 28 h.p. Lawrence "twin" created more breeze than thrust, but probably enough to fly the airplane. It would be interesting to know. *(Photo from Gerald H. Balzer Collection.)*

"Water Sprite" from Sausalito.

Sausalito is a pleasant blending of bohemian and marine influences, and a focal point for artistic talent. Its hilly terrain plunging down into the bay, and its beautiful setting from any angle contributes heavily to its past and present popularity. The houses cling precariously to the hillsides, and the town's people walk idly in the narrow streets between the buildings. Not a likely place for aircraft manufacture, one would say, but that's where the "Water Sprite" was born, and it is quite appropriate that it should be a "flying boat." Manufactured by Triton Aircraft Co. of Sausalito, California. *(A Fred Moe photo.)*

How "Skeeter" became a "Junior."

Any talk about old-timey aerial putt-putts is sure to bring up the well-known Curtiss-Wright "Junior," an airplane that had been "pushed along" its merry way through a lot of sky back in the 1930s. Stories and escapades about the "Junior" are comical and interesting, and in most cases have been told many times over, but rarely is the story told of how it all began. 'Twas said, a "Bud" Snyder had designed and built a "parasol" monoplane of wooden structure with a high-mounted "pusher engine" he called the "Buzzard" back there in 1928. A one-seater, it had been powered with various small engines. Among some of its other oddities, it used an all-movable horizontal stabilizer. Being anxious to participate in the manufacture of flivver-planes, Curtiss-Wright bought the "Buzzard" itself. It was test-flown in St. Louis by H. Lloyd Child in July of 1930. Child reported a sore lack of stability, and control was erratic at best. Pointing out that a major redesign was definitely in order!

Karl H. White, project engineer on American-izing the famous DeHaviland "Moth" biplane, was given the assignment as both Lloyd Child and Walter Beech loaned a helping hand in its development. The new design, as shown here in prototype, flew its maiden flight in October of 1930. Though its designation was model CR-1, it was mostly called the "Skeeter." Tested with a variety of small engines, the three cylinder Szekely was finally selected and the "Skeeter" was groomed for production. Now its only resemblance to the "Buzzard" is that they were both pusher-type parasol monoplanes. Slightly modified in the next few examples, the name was changed to "Junior" and the designation was now CW-1. Mass production started in March of 1931. Orders were pouring in and railroad box-cars, filled to capacity were shuttled all over the country. Of course, some were flown away from the factory. By 1932, some 270 of the "Juniors" were built and sold. It was a rare airport that did not sometime harbor at least one or two. Nearly 100 were reported to be still flying actively by 1939, and at least 15 were still flying as late as 1954. Even now there are several out there somewhere waiting to be restored. Don't pass up a ride in a Curtiss "Junior," it's a special kind of experience! *(Photo from H. Lloyd Child.)*

AIR-ISTOCRAT SP-7 - 1929 - KINNER K5

Air-Istocrat model SP-7.

Showing very little style and even less originality, the Air-Istocrat model SP-7 came upon the scene as a light parasol monoplane seating two in tandem. The ship was basically a trainer, but also suitable for the average pilot who flew just for sport. It was powered with the five cylinder Kinner K5 engine of 100 h.p., and performance was about average for this type. Oddly enough, there was 34 gallons of fuel in the wing's center-section for a range of over 500 miles! That's a long time to sit in one place. Simple in form and stout of frame, the SP-7 was apparently designed not for appeal of form and good looks, but more for trouble-free operation in hard service. Construction was robust, but quite similar to other airplanes of this type. Ship X-217H was the prototype; another SP-7 was registered as -336V. Ship X-10079 was an earlier model and powered with a five cylinder Velie M-5. A tentative price-tag for the SP-7 was $3945 at the factory. None of these were ever approved for manufacture. The builder was United States Aircraft Co. of New Brunswick, N.J. through 1928 and into 1930. *(Photo from Gerald H. Balzer Collection.)*

Reggie Sinclaire's "Eaglerock."

The big, graceful Alexander "Eaglerock" biplane, known technically as the "center-section" A-series during the late 1920s, was an airplane especially liked, and even worshiped by some! It was offered and available with just about any 90-260 h.p. engine you could get at that time. In the (ATC) approved form, the "Eaglerock" biplane was available with such engines as the ever-popular Curtiss OX-5 of 90 h.p., the "Hisso" (Hispano-Suiza) engines of 150-180 h.p., the famous J5 Wright "Whirlwind" of 220 h.p., the seven cylinder "Comet" 7D or 7E engines of 130-165 h.p., the Curtiss double-row "Challenger" engine of 170-185 h.p., and later the new 165 h.p. Wright J6-5 engine, and even the five cylinder Kinner K5 engine of 100 h.p. Some of these combinations were more popular than others, but that was the buyer's choice.

The one-of-a-kind versions that were custom-built mounted the thundering nine cylinder air-cooled Menasco-Salmson of 230-260 h.p., the earlier Wright J4B of 200 h.p., the nine cylinder Ryan-Siemens (Siemens-Halske) engine of 125 h.p., the rare 120 h.p. Jacobs and Fisher, the early seven cylinder (115 h.p.) Floco engine, the 110 h.p. Warner "Scarab," the rare seven cylinder (130 h.p.) Hallet engine, and of course the 10 cylinder double-row (French) Anzani engine of 110-120 h.p. which found its way onto so many airplanes in this country before we began developing our own! The engine-airplane combination shown here was the pride and joy of one "Reggie" Sinclaire of Colorado, a well-known pilot in the area for many years, and a former member of the Lafayette Flying Corps in France during World War I. For reasons of his own, he installed an old-timey six cylinder water-cooled Curtiss C6 engine of 160 h.p. The intricate C6 had been a respected powerplant in its time, but it required special care. Reggies "Eaglerock" was X-7187 as serial #610 and it operated in the experimental category. It was an unlikely installation, but it performed well. *(Photo from Gerald H. Balzer Collection.)*

COLUMBIA TRIAD CAL-2 - 1928 - WRIGHT J5C

"Triad" — the three-in-one airplane.

The Columbia "Triad" convertible amphibian of 1928, a three-in-one airplane, was a rather novel design built by Columbia Air Liners, Inc. of New York City. Charles A. Levine, noted trans-Atlantic voyager who flew the ocean to Germany in 1927 with Clarence Chamberlin, was the firm's financial backer and also its president. Designed on a come-apart principle whereby the hull (slipper type) or main float, could be detached leaving it as a typical landplane, or with hull installed and landing gear removed, it became a seaplane. With hull and landing gear both attached, it became an amphibian. It was now a craft that could operate both off land or water. Thus, fully equipped, the "Triad" was actually three airplanes in one! A point strongly stressed in company ads, and in its promotion.

Powered with the celebrated Wright "Whirlwind" J5C engine of 220 h.p. the ship carried up to four passengers and a pilot, with commendable performance in any of its three configurations. Or, so they said. Easily detached, the main float or hull was metal covered displacing enough area to float the loaded airplane, but we question a lack of tip-floats to keep the wing from heeling into the water. Standing very tall, its length was about 33 ft. and its width spanned nearly 50 ft. As an amphibian, it was quite heavy, so its gross

weight was nearly two tons! Built in three examples (X-305E, X-306E, and X-307E as serial #101, 102, 103) the "Triad" was variously powered with the Wright J5, the 225 h.p. Packard "Dieserl," and also the new nine cylinder Wright J6-9-300 of 300 h.p. It looked like it was going to make a go of it, but the crippling business depression of 1929 pigeon-holed any further development, and no other examples were built. Once the object of someone's pride, hopes, and rosy dreams, the versatile "Triad" (that could have been) is now only a fleeting mention in the nearly-forgotten records of airplane development. *(A Court Commercial Photo.)*

FERNIC TANDEM WING T-9 - 1929 - WRIGHT J5

Fernic did not solve the "canard" principle.

The "canard" principle and its mysteries has been pretty well solved by now, especially by one Burt Rutan who has shown near-genius in the many designs he has created. But, back in 1928-29, designers were still groping for ways to make this elusive principle safe and practical.

The interesting machine shown here was the Fernic "Tandem-Wing" T-9 as built by the Fernic Aircraft Corp. of Staten Island, New York. Loaded with such advanced features as cantilever wings, tricycle landing gear, fully cowled engines, and careful streamlining, just by looks it showed great promise. For twin-engine safety it was powered with two nine cylinder Wright "Whirlwind" J5 engines of 220 h.p. each swinging the new "Micarta" propellers. Why the airplane was built so large, and so intricate just to test an elusive principle is a puzzle. It is plain to see that it was carefully designed and well engineered, but sadly enough, it crashed and killed Fernic on its very first flight! *(Photo from Gerald H. Balzer Collection.)*

AMERICAN EAGLE - KINNER C5

Jean LaRene delivers an "American Eagle."

Kinner Motors had always worked closely with American Eagle Aircraft of Kansas City. So, when Kinner was ready to flight-test the early version of the big five cylinder "C5" engine (rated then at 190 h.p.), they selected a special modification of the "Phaeton" (an A-251 Special) for the installation. The A-251 Special registered X-285N was sort of a cross between the standard Wright-powered (R-540) "Phaeton" and the Kinner-powered model "201." In itself it was a ship that had borrowed the better features from each airplane, plus a few innovations of its own, but the design was not pursued beyond this one experimental example. So, too bad, some say it was perhaps the best "American Eagle" biplane ever built!

After the new sport biplane was duly tested at the "Eagle" factory, and cleared for service, it was up to Miss Jean LaRene to make the shake-down delivery to the Kinner Airplane and Motor Co. in California. Miss LaRene, a talented lady-pilot, had made several "American Eagle" deliveries already while employed at the airplane plant; she also participated in several national air-races and air-derbies during this period. Kinner Motors continued development of this big five cylinder engine, and it finally became the approved model C5 rated at 210 h.p. The engine was later used by several manufacturers, but it had some nasty habits and did not become a very successful powerplant. *(A Cresswell Photo.)*

An over-the-doorway sign seen at a small government weather station: "This is a Non-Prophet Organization."

AIRMASTER YOUNGSTER - 1928 - LE BLOND 60

The Ohio "Youngster."

Sparked by the enthusiasm of the "Lindbergh Era," a group of local folks got together and planned to build themselves an airplane. Why not, nearly everyone else was doing it, and they at least had good reason. In this case the Ohio Aero School of Youngstown, Ohio formed a manufacturing division (Ohio Aero Manufacturing Corp.) and students in the school were tutored in how to build an airplane. Joseph W. Esch, a pilot for years, designed the airplane in 1927-28 along usual lines and methods of construction. The building of the airplane was entrusted to the students and to Wayne Miller, the production manager, "Jud" Yoho of the Yoho and Hooker Lumber Co. in Youngstown bank-rolled the project and became president of the company.

Working both day and night classes in the school, the students (including one young lady) finally had the first airplane (-7200 as serial #AY-3) built and it was rolled out expectantly for its first hop. "Joe" Esch, though still on crutches from an earlier minor crackup, flew the Ohio "Youngster" successfully on it maiden flight. 'Tis said he was quite enthusiastic with its performance and its general behavior. Everyone had crowded together outside to see it fly!

As first tested the little "Youngster" (also called "Airmaster" was powered with a six cylinder (French) Anzani engine of some 60 h.p., but a second airplane (X-7872 as serial #AY-4) was soon after built with the five cylinder LeBlond 60 engine (as shown here) to sell for $2875 at the factory. Several inquiries about the airplane were received, and now and then, someone came out to see it, but it had not yet received its (ATC) approval for manufacture. For whatever reason, the project eventually lost most of its initial drive, and the second "Youngster/Airmaster" was sold to someone in Canada in 1929.

"Jud" Yoho still kept the first airplane for his own use. A third "Youngster/Airmaster" (-568K as serial #AY-5) was also built later on, but operational data and its disposition are unknown; in 1936 it was up for sale at $200. Seating two side-by-side, the neat little ship greatly resembled a scaled-down Mahoney-Ryan "Brougham" even to its burnished metal work. Reportedly, it was a pleasant airplane, but alas, the countryside was flooded with nice little airplanes at this time! Put this one down as another project that didn't go much beyond an exercise for a bunch of eager-to-learn students who thought they could really make it in aviation. Incidentally, Cessna Aircraft later used the name "Airmaster" for its improved line of cantilever-winged monoplanes. (Photo from Gerald H. Balzer Collection.)

GREAT LAKES 2-T-1A BIPLANE - 1930

Flying over Cleveland, Ohio!

One nice thing about flying over Cleveland, Ohio was that you could always tell which way the wind was blowing, and how strong. The airplane shown above it all was the sassy "Great Lakes" 2-T-1 biplane which was built in Cleveland. Charlie Meyers, company test-pilot is shown here testing the 2-T-1 on "Edo" floats. The little biplane did well, but it couldn't pass the spin-test with floats on at full gross load, so it was never certificated for use as a seaplane. *(Photo from Charles W. Meyers Collection.)*

Powered by Johnson "Sea Horse!"

In the long ago of the 1920s, there was no such thing as a practical aircraft engine for the light airplane. So, light-plane builders were forced to use just about anything that could be made to turn a propeller. Two cylinder and four cylinder motorcycle engines, and small automobile engines were among the first to be reworked and modified for airplane use. Occasionally, an old "Lawrance Twin" or the older three cylinder (French) Anzani were still used, but their lack of reliability kept the boys pretty close to the airport most of the time. The high-winged single-seater shown here, a true home-built project, was the "Heinemann Special," believed to be the first airplane powered with an outboard motor-boat engine. In this case, as 32 h.p. (two cycle) Johnson "Sea Horse."

Gernet Heinemann of Bellingham, Washington, a young engineering student at the University of Washington, designed this machine around the best part of a Heath "Parasol." The fast-turning "Sea Horse" engine had to be geared down to swing a larger propeller for more efficient thrust. The landing gear then had to be extended for proper ground clearance. The powerplant assembly was cowled in neatly and a nose-type radiator was provided for the water-cooled engine. Reportedly, the airplane was flown frequently at Tacoma, Washington and apparently it operated very well. Weighing only some 300 lbs. empty, we can assume that it performed quite well with this engine and this amount of power. We don't recall, nor can find evidence of any more "outboard motor" powered airplanes after this one. But, the idea was tried again in 1957 or thereabouts by Ray Stits, also an innovator, who tried it with an "Evinrude." *(Photo from Gerald H. Balzer Collection.)*

PROTOTYPE ARROW SPORT - 1926 - ANZANI 35 HP

The "Arrow Sport" in prototype.

The little "Arrow Sport" biplane surely did go straight to the hearts of American pilots, but it was not always so, especially at its beginnings! Swen Swanson, who had several good designs already in service, including the charming little "Lincoln Sport," was intrigued by a (German) Fokker D-7 they had in the shop for a rebuild. The D-VII of World War I vintage had cantilever wing panels, and theoretically required no interplane bracing of any kind. Swanson liked the idea, so he designed the prototype for the "Arrow Sport" in the same manner, and it looked pretty good to him! But, the unstrutted feature was greeted quickly with some skepticism. So, reluctantly, they added wing struts to forestall uneasiness that pilots felt when they saw all that daylight between the two wing panels!

The little prototype, as shown, was powered with a three cylinder (French) Anzani engine of some 35 doubtful horse-power, and although lively enough with only a pilot aboard, it had disconcerting tendencies to bog down with two in the side-by-side cockpit. In practice, the proto "Sport" was nothing more than a single-place airplane. And, though Joe Lowry had fun with it as a test-pilot, he found no long lines of pilots waiting eagerly to fly it! In fact, it took a little coaxing. Realizing that lack of power would be the downfall of this promising design, the "Sport" of 1927-28 was fitted with a six cylinder Anzani engine of some 60 h.p. which helped considerably. Shopping around for a more suitable airplane engine, even the five cylinder Detroit "Air Cat" was tried. When the five cylinder LeBlond "60" was introduced, and mounted in a later version of the "Sport" it was deemed especially suitable on all counts and would become the standard powerplant for production versions to follow.

With 60 h.p. now in its frame, the "Sport" was adequate for average flying around the patch, and maybe a little bit beyond, but it was no great charger as some pilots were coming to expect. So, a "pursuit-version" was planned using the five cylinder Kinner K5 engine of 90-100 h.p. With this power it became a much better airplane, a much better performing airplane, but the horse-power race as practiced by other manufacturers still left even the "Sport Pursuit" trailing behind. The "Arrow Sport" was a good-looking airplane and had charisma right from the beginning. It had a kind of appeal to pilots, despite its little shortcomings, and many of those who got to know it well remember it fondly. There were perhaps 71 of the LeBlond powered versions built, and some 24 or so of the Kinner-powered "Sport Pursuit" version, before the creeping business-depression forced the company to give up and close its doors! but, that was not yet the end of Arrow Aircraft; by operating an airport and an aeronautical trade-school, they managed to rough it through the worst part of the 1933-34-35 period, and by 1936-37 were back in business with another "Arrow Sport!" But then, that's another story. *(Photos from "Tex" Lowry Collection.)*

Some of the early "Arrow" personnel.

ZENITH ALBATROSS - 1928 - 3 SIEMENS-HALSKE SH-12 128 HP

Zenith "Albatross" had its ups and downs!

There were a lot of new and exciting airplanes coming out, one after another, in the frantic period of 1927-28. And, it was hard not to notice the Zenith "Albatross" because it was one of the world's largest land-planes. The name "Albatross" was picked perhaps to imply the grace and beauty of flight. Charles Rocheville, top-notch pilot and a pretty good eyeball engineer, flew the graceful "tri-motor" on its maiden flight early in 1928; the ship's potential was reviewed with mixed feelings.

Finding the "till" about empty of finances after the huge airplane was finally built, the Zenith group decided to use the airplane for a proposed endurance flight. This was a method to attract new investors and hopefully some sponsors. After three aborted attempts, each cut short because of various piddly engine failures, the big ship "was in hock" and had to be put up for sale. A group of Guatemalan investors was reported to have bought the big "dud," and hired Jimmie Angel, a noted gypsy-pilot and soldier-of-fortune, to try again for the endurance record. And, once again these new attempts had failed, and failed miserably!

The huge "Albatross" was originally powered with three, nine cylinder Siemens-Halske SH-12 (German-made) engines of 128 h.p. each; one wonders how it was they expected a total of 384 h.p. to fly this big airplane! The deep fuselage was nearly 50 ft. long, and the broad wing spanned some 90 ft. For the endurance flights it was reported that 1300 gals. of fuel was on board; that's enough (nearly 8000 lbs.) to break the back of any good airplane. After some more tests, Jimmie Angel found the bewildered "Albatross" very listless and woefully under-powered, so he arranged to have three seven cylinder (California-built) Axelson engines of 150 h.p. each installed. It was rumored around, and it is quite likely, these engines like the previous Siemens-Halske engines, were on consignment or lend-lease. Incidentally, as one might guess, the brave "Axelsons" did nothing to improve the airplane's performance.

A California steel-products company was sponsoring the manufacture of an air-cooled radial engine called the Western "Enterprise." Three of these engines were also tried on the "Albatross" without much more success. Believe it or not (it doesn't stop here), they also tried three of the new MacClatchie "Panther" engines. After the endurance trials had all failed, an attempt was made to ferry the huge tri-motor to Guatemala — oddly enough, this final attempt fizzled out also!

Meanwhile, aviation progress forged on ahead, and left the unlucky "Albatross" behind. Sitting woefully in storage for many years, the ill-fated giant airplane reappeared as an attraction for a Los Angeles-area gasoline station! Eventually it weathered badly and was hauled off for scrap, literally in tatters! The people connected with it at various times had all dispersed to other places, and other ventures. The Zenith Aircraft Corp. was originally in Santa Ana, California and then in nearby Midway City. The big "Albatross" in a roundabout way, had the dubious honor of being the progenitor of the lovely "Emsco" (E. M. Smith Co.) line of airplanes. This was a line of good-looking airplanes in an array of models that couldn't get past the damage of a crippling "depression." *(Photos from Stephen J. Hudek Collection.)*

ZENITH ALBATROSS - 1928

Cliff Jackson and a rare "Buhl" prototype.

Pictured is young "Cliff" Jackson who was a junior-engineer at Buhl Aircraft of Marysville, Michigan. Ettienne Dormoy, who presided over the engineering department like a "maestro" of a concert orchestra, would often let his young engineers submit ideas and concepts for study and evaluation. If anything showed promise the whole crew (never more than five) would tackle the project for development. One such case was the rare little low-winged monoplane, shown with young Cliff posing nonchalantly to picture its relative size. The project was carried out quickly as a good exercise in airplane design and development. Evaluation of the test-flown prototype had soon proven that the depression-ridden aviation industry of the 1930s certainly didn't need another sporty, two-seated monoplane!

The airplane, as shown, was of basically simple and rugged construction, a type that would endear itself to those that operated from little sod-covered fields. After all, this is where most of the sport-flying took place. This was a ship then, that was fashioned to take the scrapes and knocks of everyday service. The seven cylinder Warner "Scarab" engine of 110 h.p. was neatly cowled in an NACA-type fairing using novel pressure-exits for the airstream as it left the engine area. The landing gear was a rigid structure with only the roly-poly "airwheels" taking up the shocks; an "oleo gear" was to be an option. The deep cockpit for two side-by-side was roomy with a transparent side-panel on each side for better vision out. There was no record of the ship's performance, or characteristics, but it wasn't scrapped, so perhaps it was considered worthwhile. Records show that Cliff Jackson later inherited this airplane — perhaps as a part of his unpaid wages when Buhl Aircraft finally folded up. *(Photo from W. U. Shaw.)*

CURTISS-REID RAMBLER - 1929 - WRIGHT-GIPSY 90 HP

Curtiss-Reid "Rambler" didn't make it in America.

As if Curtiss didn't already have enough to keep them busy, they decided to purchase control of the Reid Aircraft Co., Ltd. of Canada in 1928. This to give them access to the Canadian market. Curtiss-Reid Aircraft was formed in December of 1928 in Montreal with highly-ambitious plans for building 250 of the "Rambler" sport-trainers per year. The prototype airplane was flown in September of 1928, and production versions followed soon after. Many problems were encountered with early machines, but modifications to the control system and wing-folding mechanism were made in subsequent airplanes. The "Rambler" as powered with the English "Cirrus" engine finally blossomed into a pretty fair little airplane. One Curtiss-Reid "Rambler" (NC-661W) as shown here, had an American-built "Wright-Gipsy" engine of 90 h.p. installed, and was exported to the Curtiss-Wright Flying Service on Long Island. It was delivered in April of 1931, but was soon damaged in an accident. The broken "Rambler" was repaired, but when it had another accident in August of the same year, it was written off as a bad investment!

The "Rambler" biplane went through several model updates in Canada, and pilots liked it well enough, but it was rated less favorably than the popular D. H. "Moth" which had established a good reputation. W. T. Reid and Martin Berlyn, former Canadian-Vickers engineers, had designed and developed that folding wing "Rambler," but by the time they had fashioned it into a pretty fair airplane the depression of the 1930s had started. What sales and orders there were had soon virtually dried up. Curtiss-Reid hung on for a while as best it could, but was finally forced into bankruptcy in 1932. They spent large sums of money preparing an airport, building a factory, and developing the airplane — it simply did not pay off! Montreal Aircraft Industries, Ltd. was then formed to take over the assets. *(Photo from Gerald H. Balzer Collection.)*

EASTMAN E2 SEA ROVER - 1929 - CHALLENGER 170-185

"Sea Rover" lands in the snow.

Back in the winter of 1929 a daring pilot purposely landed this Eastman "Sea Rover," as shown, on the snow-covered tarmac of the Grosse Ille Airport in the wintry land of Michigan. The oddity of it was that the "Rover" pictured is a genuine flying-boat and had no wheels! This was, of course, a factory-sponsored test to see if emergency landings could actually be made without wheels if need be. Also, to see if the hull was stout enough to take this kind of unusual treatment. Tests did prove the plane's hull and airframe were indeed quite strong enough to endure the wallop of a forced landing on various conditions of terra-firma. But, Jim Eastman was later fearful that other hot-shot pilots might purposely try it too. Needless to say, this nagging worry hastened design and development, and they soon introduced a set of retractable wheels for the sea-going "Sea Rover." This add-on made it into an amphibian, and now it could operate from water, and land also.

The sporty "Sea Rover" was built in Detroit in small number by the Eastman Division of the Detroit Aircraft Corp. It was designed especially for the well-to-do water-loving sportsman-pilot. The E-2 seated three or four depending on how hippy they were. In areas such as Detroit, or lower Michigan for that matter, a place that was strewn with countless lakes and several large rivers, one could enjoy hours of carefree flying just rubber-necking the lovely scenery. Or too, drop in to visit various water-front parks and resorts. Hanging snugly from the upper wing in a tractor-fashion, was a six cylinder Curtiss "Challenger" engine of 170-185 h.p. Performance was good enough for a flying-boat, a craft most always penalized by some extra weight and surely a lot more drag.

Later in 1930 the E-2-A version of this craft was introduced with a retractable landing gear; this wheeled unit was available also as a retro-fit for all previously built "Rover" flying-boats. This installation could set you back by about a thousand bucks, but it proved to be well worth it. Selling fairly well for about $10,000 each, the fun-loving "Rover" was soon confronted with the infamous, crippling depression, and the market for this type of sport-plane just disappeared! It behooves one to consider occasionally that this type of airplane could very well be resurrected. Being in the cockpit of a breezy flying-boat high over water is an interesting and soothing kind of fun that tends to make earth-bound problems disappear. *(Photo from Gerald H. Balzer Collection.)*

In a lagoon at Belle Isle.

GREENWOOD-YATES GEODETIC - 1935

Greenwood-Yates was weaved like a basket!

This twin-engined cutie shown was the Greenwood-Yates, an unusual exercise in "geodetic" construction. The lower photo shows why it was often called "basket-weave." The theory behind this type of construction was the fact that no single member was that critical to the structure's integrity. In fact, large gaping holes could be poked through anywhere, and it would still hold together — the distribution of stresses would divert strains around a break, or hole, in the structure and not let it fail.

The airplane as shown completed was the "Bi-Craft," an all-wood machine with fabric cover that seated two in tandem. More odd perhaps than its type of construction was the fact that it was a "twin" powered with two four cylinder (flat-four) Continental A-40 engines of some 40 h.p. each. There is

such a thing as twin-engine safety, but this wouldn't be it. It's doubtful if 40 h.p. would fly it! Built in Oregon during 1934-35 (when Oregon was a literal hot-bed of home-built activity), the "twin" was put together by Allan D. Greenwood and George Yates; whether they designed it is not known. It later mounted two flat-four Menasco M-50 engines of 50 h.p. each. No doubt it was an interesting fun project, but no data was found on its use or disposition. *(Photos from Gerald H. Balzer Collection.)*

MATTLEY FLIVVER-PLANE - 1931 - CONTINENTAL A-40

The Mattley "Flivver-Plane."

There is doubt that introduction of the Mattley "Flivver-Plane" in 1930 was any cause for celebration, but perhaps it was a noticeable event in San Bruno where it was reportedly built. Looking very much like a shop project hurriedly put together by eager students, the FP (Flivver-Plane) could not boast of much else beyond simplicity, and a promised very low purchase price. Of course, everybody and his brother was building flivver-planes at this time, and their creators were more often driven by enthusiasm rather than good sense. Luckily, out of this period came airplanes such as the Aeronca C-2/C-3 and the Taylor "Cub." The rest of the guys out there sorta lost out, but they all had fun trying.

Among the first to use the newly-introduced Continental A-40, a flat-four engine of 38 h.p., the early "Mattley" FP seated one or two. First record of a Mattley was an FP-1 (10615) as serial #6, then an FP-2 (12707) as serial #7. So, at least these two were built, and perhaps more. The FP-2 was listed as a two-place with side-by-side seating. Henry Mattley was general manager of the firm, and Lynn Harp was chief engineer. The Mattley was around for several years; some say as late as 1935. *(Photo from Gerald H. Balzer Collection.)*

The "General" gets a job at Wright Aero.

This very imposing airplane was the so-called "Mailplane" model 107. General Airplanes Corp. was already building the "Aristocrat" 102 series, and felt there would be a demand for the big "107" in the airmail and air-cargo end of air transport, both here and abroad. Built mostly of metals in monocoque and cantilever construction, the Hornet-powered "107," for a time, was the largest single-engined mailplane in the U.S.A. Needless to say, there was no demand for an airplane of this type at this (1929-30) time. Despite all its qualifications, the one-only "Mailplane" was relegated to being a hangar-queen for a while, while waiting for someone to buy it. As if destiny required the proud "107" to prove itself in actual work, the ship was finally acquired by Wright Aeronautical at Caldwell, New Jersey for flight-testing their new line of 1000 h.p. "Cyclone" engines. All prototype "G" engines were tested in the "General," as well as the first twin-row Wright that became the famous R-2600 engine of World War II. It was a blessing for the proud "107" to be put to work by Wright Engines where it apparently did an admirable job.

This beautiful airplane was a gathering of innovations for its time, a mix that set it apart from the norm in many ways — it certainly suffered from bad timing. The years 1929-31 were poor times to launch the career of a new airplane, no matter its role, and especially one committed to cargo-hauling. General Airplanes had already struck-out with the twin-engined "Surveyor" that didn't seem to fit anywhere, the "Cadet" trainer received only a luke-warm welcome, and the "Aristocrat" was having tough-sledding too. So, General Airplanes were just hanging on by their finger-nails! In 1930 General left Buffalo to more modest facilities on Roosevelt Field on Long Island. As to the "107," it operated through 1937 and was scrapped just prior to World War II. *(Photo from Stephen J. Hudek Collection.)*

The first home-made airplane in Hawaii.

Aviation received quite a boost in the "Islands" when the "Dole Derby" fliers, Art Goebel and Martin Jensen, landed safely on Hawaii in late 1927. Though it had been a rather tragic "race," causing several needless casualties, yet it did acquaint many people with the airplane, and sparked interest in the wonders of flying. Except for routine flights by the U.S. military, for years there was very little commercial and private flying in the Hawaiian Islands. But, in a few years after the "Dole" race, there was increasing acceptance of the airplane as a means of transport, business, and even sport.

Because of the great distance from the mainland, and because everything had to be shipped in, not many production airplanes had been brought over. It was far easier to order a "kit" and build your own airplane from scratch. That's just what Glenn Belcher did. He ordered a kit of the popular Henderson-powered Heath "Parasol," building it in his basement by stages during spare time for about $750. Shown here at the John Rodgers Airport in Honolulu was the first home-made airplane built in Hawaii. It was formally christened in December of 1929 with a bottle of milk! Glenn Belcher, proud of his self-built airplane, named it "Miss Barbara" after his 22-month-old daughter, who he was also proud of. Not much else is known, but it's almost certain young Belcher had fun flying over "Hawaiian Paradise" with his home-built Heath "Parasol." *(Photo by Hawaiian News Bureau.)*

COMMECIAL AIRCRAFT SUNBEAM C-1 - 1929 - WRIGHT J6-9-300

Elinor and Bobbie keep the "Sunbeam" up for 45 hours.

Bobbie Trout and Elinor Smith, both accomplished young lady-pilots, who had already set several record flights that put them in the lime-light, were chatting idly one day in Cleveland during the National Air Races. Among other things, they talked about getting together someday soon to set a refueled-in-the-air endurance record for women, which would be a first. It was Bobbie Trout in California (who was just 23) who got the equipment rounded up, and the backing for the proposed flight. She wired Elinor Smith (who was going on 18) to hurry up and come out west.

The endurance-ship was the little-known "Sunbeam Commercial," an odd cabin biplane (similar to the one shown here) which was powered with a nine cylinder Wright J6-9-300 engine of 300 h.p. Its stripped cabin area was crammed full of fuel tanks, connected together with assorted plumbing. The refueling-tanker was a lumbering old Liberty-powered (ex-NAT) Curtiss "Carrier Pigeon," that surely had seen better days. Because the two airplanes were so unmatched in speed and other characteristics, and because the "Sunbeam" was said to be about as stable as a roller-coaster, this created problems in getting a good hook-up for the refueling. Unbridled credit must surely go to young Elinor Smith who was the pilot during all refueling contacts, and to Bobbie Trout who handled the dangling hose from the "tanker." Both of the young ladies had jobs that really tested their talents, and their behavior under stress! Under the circumstances, it is quite likely that both airplanes were operated mostly by instinct!

After some practice flights of 10 to 18 hours each, the ladies took off one morning early for a crack at setting a first-ever record. They were sponsored in part by Richfield Oil who provided all the gasoline, and Kendall Oil who provided oil for the engine. After passing 36 hours in the air over the Los Angeles area, things looked pretty good. But then, they failed to take on a full load on one of the hook-ups with the bouncing "Pigeon," because its tired old "Liberty" engine sputtered, coughed, and finally conked out! This short-load would surely shorten their time in the air if the "Pigeon" did not get back up in time, which it didn't. Consequently, the engine on the "Sunbeam" ran out of fuel and sputtered to a stop fairly near its home base, so daring little Elinor made a rather hairy dead-stick landing at night to end the eventful flight.

In all respects, it had been a harrowing flight. Both Smith and Trout were bruised and tired, and disappointed in not staying up for the 168 hours as planned. But under the trying circumstances it was a job very well done by a couple of young ladies who proved they had "the stuff." Of course, it didn't take long for the record they made to be broken, everyone expected that. But by then, both Bobbie Trout and Elinor Smith had went their separate ways to take on other challenges in the exciting world of woman in aviation. The "Sunbeam" biplane was lucky to have had its day in the lime-light for a time, and lucky too to have made a few headlines in the papers. As everyone went on to other things, the plane was soon forgotten, and probably it's just as well. *(Photo from Gerald H. Balzer Collection.)*

Learning to fly at night?

Finally realizing that many potential students stayed away from his flying-school because the pressure of their jobs kept them busy during the daytime, a local flying-school operator with time on his hands was mulling over the possibility of teaching students to fly at night. Like on their off-times, he says, late in the evening, or even at night? Why not?

The air traffic was much lighter, the night air was always cooler and smoother, and flying was really more of a pleasure. When the word got around, several aspiring students inquired and a few offered to give it a try. Surprisingly, it worked out very well.

One local aspirant, more eager than the rest, signed up early for the course, and soon found it very much to his liking. In due time, and some eight hours and 40 minutes of "dual" later he was asked to "solo," and it went off without a hitch. From then on, he was out there most evenings putting in the solo-time to earn his "private." All during the darkness of night!

GREAT LAKES AMPHIBIAN - 2 WR J6-5

"Great Lakes" amphibian that tried, but couldn't.

Nearly everyone knows of, or has heard of the "Great Lakes," that sassy little swept-wing biplane that was an aerobatic champion and an air-show star for years on end. But, very few know that Great Lakes Aircraft once launched upon a sorry venture to develop a sport-type amphibian. As shown here below at the annual Detroit Air show, the cute-looking "duck" was first designed to fly with two four cylinder Cirrus "Hermes" engines of 115 h.p. each. Now then, does that sound like a reasonable request? Incidentally, it had to be freighted from Cleveland to the air-show on a flat-car because it just would not fly!

GREAT LAKES AMPHIBIAN - 2 CIRRUS HERMES 115 HP

After the showing it was later re-engined with two five cylinder Wright J6-5 engines of 150 h.p. each; and then it did fly, but just barely. Charlie Meyers, test-pilot for G.L.A.C. at the time, sadly related to the onlookers that it took up half of Lake Erie to get off with a gross load. And, it never did fly off land. Needless to say, the ship was hangared for further study and discussion, but mostly in embarrassment. In 1935 it was seen with two seven cylinder Wright J6-7 engines of 225 h.p. each, but no one will come forward to say they actually saw it fly! Meyers was asked if he participated in design of the four-seated 4-A1. He said something like, "Geez, hell no, it was all "Dick" Richardson's fault. That is, Captain Holden C. Richardson (USN), who was earlier on the Curtiss design team that fashioned the famous "NC" flying boats, of which NC-4 was perhaps the most famous. The prototype model 4-A1 and 4 uncompleted airframes of the same type were manufactured by the Great Lakes Aircraft corp. at Cleveland, Ohio. *(Photos from Charles W. Meyers and Stephen J. Hudek Collection.)*

RICHFIELD OIL CO. FOKKER F-10-A - SUPER TRI-MOTOR

"Swinging" a compass??

What the heck are all these people doing around that F-10-A Fokker "Super Tri-Motor?" And, how about that guy on top of the wing? Well, actually they are "swinging the compass" as it was done back in the 1920s. The top-of-the-line F-10-A shown was a plush-appointed version used by the Richfield Oil Co. of California for transport of executives on company business. Swinging a compass nowadays is not nearly so exciting to do or to watch! *(Photo from the Gerald H. Balzer Collection.)*

TILBURY-FUNDY FLASH - 1932 - CHURCH MARATHON 41 HP

World's smallest racing airplane.

The Tilbury-Fundy "Flash" was the world's smallest racing airplane. As shown in prototype sitting next to Victor Fleming's "Travel Air" S-6000-B, one could easily believe it. Designed by Owen Tilbury and Clarence Fundy, the "Flash" was built in Bloomington, Illinois during 1932. Built to fit Art Carnahan, he still had to take his shoes off to get in the cockpit! Up front was a neatly cowled four cylinder air-cooled inline Church "Marathon" engine of 45 h.p. Russ Hosler, famous test pilot, was engaged to make the maiden flight, but he could not get it to fly! It was painfully shy in wing area, and the tail-group was too small. The "Flash" was to be entered in the National Air Races for 1932, but now there was work to do.

Modified with a wing of greater span, and more effective area in the tail-group, the pee-wee-sized "Flash" made its debut at the Chicago races of 1933. Art Carnahan took 1st place in the 200 cu. in. class at 115 m.p.h., and a second place in a previous race. The Chicago air races were held that year over Labor Day weekend — the "Flash" again won the 200 cu. in. class event. The speedy "Flash" then raced at the National Air races held in Cleveland in 1934, and again it did well. In the winter of 1934-35, the plane and crew migrated to the air races held in Florida. Later on back to the National Air Races held at Cleveland. From here on the story gets rather fuzzy as to how the "Flash" was fairing, and then it just seemed to disappear. Some 40 years later it was found in a barn covered in dust and literally rotting away! Luckily, a group planned to restore it for display in a museum. *(Photo from Gerald H. Balzer Collection.)*

"Liberty"climbs to 17,907 feet for a record.

The "Liberty" monoplane of 1931 was perhaps not just another light airplane — some have said it could have been the "Cadillac" of the lightplane field. This is a statement volunteered by several pilots and mechanics who were familiar with it. Basically, it was built well, soundly designed, and performed a head above other airplanes of its type. It was developed on Lambert Field in St. Louis, but operations were moved to Kansas City, Kansas where facilities were more attractive. According to stories, nearly everybody that cared to had a chance to fly it, and all were duly impressed with its performance and its behavior. It certainly looked like there was a bright future ahead for the fussed-over "Liberty."

While it was being shown around at Kansas City (Fairfax Airport), Guy Poyer offered to install one of his three cylinder "Poyer" 3-45 engines into this bragged on "Liberty" monoplane. Perhaps they could set a new altitude record and get a little fame for the airplane, and the engine too. (One of the novel features of the Poyer engine was the facility to screw down the cylinder barrels to raise the compression ratio.) So, they screwed down the "jugs" a little tighter to an 8 to 1 compression ratio, dumped 7cc of tetra-ethyl (lead) fluid into each gallons of gasoline, and off they went. They had no idea what horsepower was being developed, at the time. Before the afternoon was over "Bill" Cadwell had climbed to 17,907 ft. for a new lightplane altitude record!

But alas, exuberance over the airplane's exceptional ability had later caused tragedy. "Bill" Cadwell was up "stunting" the eager "Liberty" one day, and in his enjoyment he literally broke it apart in the air! Of course, Cadwell perished in the crash. Thus, what looked like a great promise was destined to end in sadness. The sport-type "Liberty" was an open cockpit parasol monoplane with side-by-side seating for two. It was normally powered with a three cylinder Szekely SR-3-0 engine of 45 h.p. The "Poyer," by the way, could have become a great little engine, but it never reached production. *(Photos from Gerald H. Balzer Collection.)*

Surely, there have been all sorts of good and bad regulations in aviation in the past 60 years, or so. But, the one imposed on fliers over the land of Egypt back in the 1930s will certainly take the cake! All flight in Egyptian territory was to begin and end only on government approved landing grounds, or designated official airports. Absolutely no landings would be permitted anywhere else! You could, however secure a government permit for landing on unauthorized areas (like a force landing?), but only if you applied for the permit five days ahead of time. And, you must identify the time and the place of the intended landing. Needless to say, this precluded any forced landings, whether planned or unplanned. You can bet all fliers over Egypt checked their airplanes and their engines very carefully before each flight!

Aviation historians take note: Ernest Hemingway, noted author, once said to a group of literary hopefuls — "If one waits until he or she knows all there is to know about a particular subject, hardly anything would ever get written!"

Amen.

TIPTON SPORT - 1936 - WARNER SCARAB JR 90 HP

The Tipton "Sport."

In the long lineup of "only one built" airplanes was the Tipton "Sport." It seems that B. G. Tipton, who did the design work on the "Sport," had good ideas he wished to incorporate into an airplane of his own. Ideas he found lacking in other airplanes of this type. First, he stressed the importance of good all-around visibility; note the extra large window area. The leading edges and the trailing edges of the wing root were notched at the fuselage, and overhead in the cabin was a large, full-length skylight. The next consideration was better streamlining; note fully cowled radial engine, and the roundish, deeply faired fuselage, and fairing on most of the landing gear trusses. In all, the "Tipton" presented a rather neat appearance, and could keep up with any of the 90 h.p. "Monocoupes" — or, so it was said.

Stories handed down about this airplane credit B. G. Tipton with the design, and William Ostoff with the engineering and stress analysis. The ship was built over a period in 1936 by Earl C. Reed and Walter Bury, both talented airplane-builders, in Reed's airplane-repair shop in Raytown Missouri. Maestro "Ole" Fahlin carved out the propeller. Typical of the period, the fabric covered fuselage was of welded steel tubing, and the fabric-covered wing was of wooden spars and ribs. Seating two side-by-side, the interior was comfortable, easy to see out of, and handled quite well both on the ground and in the air. The five cylinder Warner "Scarab Jr." engine of 90 h.p. provided satisfying performance, and in overall assessment, the "Tipton" was a pleasure to fly. As the model W-7200X (X-16468 as serial #100), it was the only one of its kind built. Tipton Aircraft co. was formed in Kansas City for possible manufacture, but production was never realized. Operational history and final disposition is unknown. *(Photo from Earl C. Reed.)*

TAYLORCRAFT A - 1938 - 40 HP

On to Milford, Ohio — backwards!

There have been many unusual flights performed by the light airplane of yesteryear, a popular topic when pilots are hangar-flying, but this one related here is perhaps more unusual than most. On this particular wintry day in January of 1938 over Lunken Airport in Cincinnati, there was an odd combination of winds, winds which blew Northeast about 11 m.p.h. near the surface, but blew at 70 m.p.h. or more above 3000 ft. Informed of this phenomenon, three young hot-shot pilots jumped into their light-planes (all were said to be 40-horse T-Crafts), and took off to do a little "backwards flying." Grouping together in formation it was great fun for them to be flying in reverse, so they decided to do a little cross-country. Milford, Ohio which was a town in line with the way they were going was about 10 miles away, so this became their objective.

Holding their airspeed steadily at about 40 m.p.h., the three airplanes in formation were drifting backwards at about 30 m.p.h. They reached Milford in about 20 minutes, and then nosed down sharply into lighter winds for the return flight to Lunken Airport. The entire flight took about 45 minutes, and during this time no turns were made from take-off to landing; the three ships were constantly headed into a southwest heading. The 71+ m.p.h. wind at 3000 ft. and higher that day was the strongest wind aloft recorded over Cincinnati in several years! The differential between surface winds and winds aloft made this unusual flight possible. This was believed to be the first-ever backward cross-county flight ever accomplished with a formation of airplanes. The three young pilots were commended for their daring and expertise. *(Photo from Robert S. Hirsch Collection.)*

MC GAFFEY AVIATE - 1936 - FORD V-8

McGaffey's "Aviate" — "everyman's" airplane?

As shown here, the McGaffey "Aviate" was yet another contender in a frantic search for "everyman's" airplane. In the mid-thirties, this was a pet dream and a concept highly endorsed by Eugene Vidal; the government had specifications for a "$700 airplane," an airplane that just about anyone off the street could afford to buy, and to fly! A nationwide contest (which wound up as a fiasco) prompted many designs; most were unconventional. Some were powered with converted auto engines of which the "Arrow Sport" V-8 was perhaps the best known, and the most practical example. Based more or less, on the Claire Vance design of his "Viking" flying-wing, the "Aviate" offered a fuselage-pod with closed-in comfort, and was built mostly of metal, and promised reliability in hard service. The familiar radiator grille was more than a hint that it was powered with a converted 1935 Ford V-8 automobile engine of some 85 h.p.

McGaffey's airplane was variously reported in periodicals as being built in Pasadena, practically completed (May 1935) in Santa Monica, and that production was planned at Grand Central Airport in Glendale, California. A facility in Inglewood was also studied. The roomy fuselage-pod seated two side-by-side in relative comfort, and the lowered wing provided easy entry. Reports said it flew well, was robust in character, and promised to be the ideal airplane for the low-income week-end flyer. Demonstrations proved too, the "Aviate" was exceptionally stable, was easy to handle in most any situation, and could muster up a top speed of 115 m.p.h. The Prototype "Aviate" was X-14951 as serial #11, and apparently the only example that was built! Neil McGaffey provided the basic design, and F. M. Smith engineered it. Naturally, it did not meet the "$700 airplane" criteria; price quoted was $1500 at factory field. Manufactured by McGaffey Airplane Development Co. *(Photo from Gerald H. Balzer Collection.)*

The life and times of the "Rouffaer."

This mysterious little sport-cabin monoplane, shown here as a scale model, did according to published accounts finally become a real airplane. It was initially agreed, too, that this was the hush-hush "Rouffaer" R-6 (registered as X-13393) being rumored for months as a dashing two-seater of highly innovative aerodynamic form and high performance potential. The power-plant of 80 h.p. (hinted as possibly some new design) was an air-cooled "flat-four" (opposed) engine of undisclosed manufacture. At least a year or so in the making, mostly under wraps, the R-6 reportedly had finally flown a successful maiden flight, demonstrating all that was promised. But, by that time the drawn-out development endeavor had exhausted all of the available finances and much of the enthusiasm. It makes one wonder if there is anyone out there who really saw it fly!

Ken Blackwell, who was the draftsman-designer for Jan Rouffaer, and "Heini" Hendricks (all three contributed to the design of this airplane, and Marvin Martin was the engineer), soon found himself quite alone with this project, and holding the bag, so to speak. Without any fanfare, nor prior notice, Rouffaer and Hendricks (both of whom had soldier-of-fortune tendencies) had signed on with an agent to fly on contract with some developing airline in China. Thus, leaving poor Blackwell with the airplane and its destiny. There being no other choice, because no other financing could be found, the lovely airplane was finally dismantled. Various parts obtained on loan or consignment were returned to owners and suppliers. The books were then closed on the "Rouffaer" and Ken Blackwell, perhaps with a heavy heart, went on to more stable things. What structural remains were left were probably scrapped. Rouffaer Aircraft Corp. was formed in California (probably Oakland) in October of 1933. *(Photo from Gerald H. Balzer Collection.)*

World's littlest tri-motor.

For many of the early years the "tri-motor" airplane reigned as queen of the airways, and was looked upon by all as the epitome of safety and reliability in the air. That is, until it was unseated from its place on top of the heap by some brash young "twins." Airplanes such as the Boeing "247," the Lockheed (model 10) "Electra," and of course, the famous Douglas DC-2. Quite recently Boeing went back to the tri-motored configuration, as did Lockheed and so did Douglas. Perhaps we may again see the popular revival of transport airplanes with three engines.

The little jewel that prompted this discussion in the first place is the cute-as-a-bug's-ear machine shown here. Without a doubt, the smallest "tri-motor" that was ever built to this time, it was the Crawford "Sport" built by William F. Crawford in Seal Beach, California. Built early in 1928, it doesn't appear to be much over six ft. tall, perhaps some 20 ft. or so in length, and its thick cantilever wing probably spanned some 35 ft. A pity they didn't show some people standing by for comparison.

Listed as a two-to-four (?) place, the occupants sat enclosed well up front where they could watch the little three cylinder Anzani engines as they did their darndest to crank out some 35 h.p. each. Later, the plane was reportedly tested with three, three-cylinder Skekely SR-3 engines of 40 h.p. each. The entire airframe, wing and all, was of welded steel tubing covered in fabric. Otherwise normal, one innovation was the all-flying horizontal stabilizer, a method of pitch control that became popular in more recent years. Having little information on the interesting milestone in light-airplane development, it is easy to speculate that each flight in this machine must have been pure adventure! Manufactured by Crawford Motor & Airplane Manufacturing, Inc. at Seal Beach, California. *(Inman photo from Gerald H. Balzer collection.)*

ABRAMS EXPLORER - 1938 - WRIGHT R-975-E 330 HP

Abrams "Explorer" somewhere over Pennsylvania.

Talbert Abrams, a well-known Michigan pilot, and a pioneer in aerial photography, formed Abrams Aerial Survey in 1925 at Lansing, Michigan. Like others dabbling in the relatively new field, he was unable to find an airplane particularly suitable for taking clear, sharp photographs from the air. For more than 10 years Abrams tried various aircraft for mapping and photo-work. Some he found were better than others, but none was really ideal for his purpose. They all had their shortcomings for this type of work.

As aerial mapping and aerial photography swelled into a business of considerable proportion, it was logical to assume it would be practical to design and build special airplanes. Airplanes that surely could be better fit to do the job. The rigid requirements of an airplane especially designed to do aerial photography, or large scale mapping, without compromise, dictated a special shape to fit the function. Armed with his own "specs" for the new airplane, a list prompted by over 10 years in the business, Abrams got together with talented Kenneth Ronan, a former Stinson engineer. The design work began in 1936, and the Abrams Aircraft Corp. was formed in October of 1937.

Appropriately named the "Explorer," the airplane took its shape as it embodied the many innovations particularly suited for the rigors of high-altitude mapping, and various styles of aerial photography. Hence, the "greenhouse" in front for maximum visibility, with the engine mounted in back for less noise and vibration. A special-purpose airplane, the "Explorer" provided a stable platform of exceptional visibility, with performance and range tailored to extensive mapping at altitudes up to 27,000 ft. Oxygen was carried for any jobs over 10,000 ft. Walter J. Carr, another famous Michigan pilot, and builder of the "Cabinaire," flew the "Explorer" on its maiden flight sometime in the latter part of 1937. Carr, it was said, was enthused with the ship's abilities, and gave it good marks, but hinted that added horsepower would unleash more of the airplane's latent performance. First powered with a nine cylinder Wright R-975-E engine of 330 h.p., mounted in pusher-fashion, the craft was later powered with the newer (supercharged) 420 h.p. Wright R-975-E3 engine. The extra power provided significant gains in all-around performance, especially at high altitude.

The striking airplane was show-cased around the country making appearances at the national air-races, regional airshows, and it did a good bit of Abram's own work. Onlookers were enthused and voice flattering comments, but no one seemed interested enough in the concept to put in an order for a similar airplane. Perhaps it was too far ahead of its time, an obvious break from the norm which fostered skepticism, or perhaps there were still lingering effects from the crippling depression that had set the 1930s economy on its ear. Eventually, even with all its tailored innovations, the "Explorer" found itself outpaced by the march of events. It was then donated to the Smithsonian Institution for display in the National Air Museum; there to stand as another significant milestone in the relentless flow of progress in aviation. *(Photos from Gerald H. Balzer Collection.)*

Abrams shows various cameras used in "Explorer."

BEN JONES S-125 - 1937 - MENASCO C4-125

The racy-looking S-125 by Ben Jones, Inc.

Ben Jones, well-known eastern operator who tried to revive the graceful "New Standard" biplane with only a little success, produced parts for 10 complete airplanes in 1937 on a Group 2 approval numbered 2-542. From the pile of assorted parts, five were assembled and sold as the "Jones-Standard" D-25. Five that could have become airplanes were not assembled because there was no interest out there for this type of airplane any more. During this time and somewhat earlier, Jones had also been engaged in the development of a racy-looking small cantilever sport monoplane called simply the model S-125. The unique S-125 was developed from an idea he came up with in 1935. Construction was more or less conventional for the time, but its aerodynamic form was far from ordinary. It is at once obvious that the designer drew heavily from the popular racing-airplane influence.

Especially unusual, even for this time, was the stout, tapered cantilever (internally braced) wing, a neat spatted landing gear quite similar to that on the famous Northrop "Gamma," and a sliding canopy over the two occupants seated in tandem. For a slim waist and low frontal area it was powered with a four cylinder air-cooled, inverted inline Menasco C4-125 engine of 125 h.p. The wing span was a graceful 31 ft., and the length was a slender 24 ft. Weight empty was 1125 lbs., and the gross weight was 2000 lbs., providing a generous amount for the payload allowance. All this would surely seem like the ingredients needed for a sport-utility airplane with near-super performance. In fact, *"a m.p.h. for every h.p."* was part of the company's sales pitch, and many believed it when they saw the airplane.

BEN JONES S-125 - 1937 - MENASCO C4-125

On the way to take-off!

Everything looked just fine on the airplane's formal debut one day early in 1937, but it is sad to say, the nifty little S-125, despite all its charm and good taste, was almost destroyed on its attempt at a maiden flight! Most reports say that the aileron controls were crossed causing the speeding airplane to heel over unexpectedly as it became airborne, and it crashed, embarrasing everybody! Proper preflight inspection surely would have avoided such a calamity as this.

Unhappily, Jones was not too keen on the idea of rebuilding the airplane, or to partake into any further development. On the verge of being financially strapped, Jones offered the five uncompleted D-25 airframes for sale along with the manufacturing rights. The as-is S-125 apparently came along with the deal made to White Airplane Co. of LeRoy, New York. The S-125 (which should have been given a nice catchy name) was originally registered as NX-16791 (serial #1) as manufactured by Ben Jones, Inc. on the Schenectady County airport in Schenectady, New York. Some reports (probably more like a rumor) say the S-125 was rebuilt and presented for government approval, but no certificate was ever issued. *(Photos from Gerald H. Balzer Collection.)*

A sign seen posted in a U.S. Army Air Corps. parachute shop back in the 1930s — **"YOU CAN DEPEND ON US TO LET YOU DOWN!"**

CROSS-FOSTER CF-1 - WARNER 110

Cross-Foster was object of a lawsuit.

From the stories told about this rare little airplane, it is entirely possible that it made a lot more money for its developers by not being produced beyond a prototype. Looking back, it is quite probable it would have lost money had it been certificated and put into production. Such was the peculiar fate and circumstance of the Cross-Foster CF-1, a low-winged sport monoplane. It poses here as an open sport two-seater of updated construction that was supposed to embody several nifty innovations in metal airplane construction. The overall design was mostly by Jack E. Foster, a design-engineer and capable pilot, formerly with American Eagle Aircraft and a while with Rearwin Airplanes. The project was financed by Dr. Walter Cross who loved to dabble with airplanes, and especially with new airplane designs.

Cross & Foster had collaborated a few years earlier on the twin-engined "American Eagle" model A-529, an airplane that had missed the point and wound up in the scrap heap early on. Later confronted with the business-depression that had just about crippled most airplane manufacturers in the 1930s, Cross & Foster peered into the future of airplane design and aircraft fabrication — all-metal airplanes were surely to be the future, and their airplane was to be one of the first in line. Labeled the model CF-1, their little low-winged monoplane did embody the latest in (known and experimental) all-metal technique. Its outstanding feature was a patented cantilever wing design, and it was probably the first airplane to use cast aluminum rivets.

Built in Kansas City, Missouri in a spare corner of Earl Reed's big hangar, it shaped up nicely with a smooth semi-monocoque fuselage and a sturdy tapered cantilever (internally braced) wing. The prototype seated two side-by-side out in the open (a canopy was planned as an option), and it was powered with the ever-popular seven cylinder Warner "Scarab" engine of 110-125 h.p. which provided a more than adequate performance. A speed-ring (Townend ring) engine cowl was to be offered to fair-in the engine. The landing gear was primarily used in the fixed position for tests, but it was designed to be retractable. The Cross-Foster was test-flown several times during 1930-31, and the general handling was reported to be good, but it stalled viciously and did have "poor spin characteristics." This failing, making pilots uneasy, probably could have been overcome with some modifications. But, more than $30,000 had been spent already, so the project was set aside for the time being. It was stashed in the back of Blaine Tuxhorn's hangar, along with several other hangar-queens where it spent the next several years. While sitting here in neglect, it collected a liberal coating of hangar-dust and several layers of pigeon droppings. (What an inglorious retirement for a rather nice airplane.)

Cross & Foster had later found out that Douglas Aircraft had infringed on some of their wing patents when developing their commercial DC-series. The resulting squabble and lawsuit was said to have eventually provided a liberal settlement whereby Dr. Cross had recovered his initial investment in development of the airplane, with a tidy sum left over! Nearly all who knew of the CF-1 project, agreed that had it been certificated, gone into production, and put up for sale, it probably would have made far less money than the settlement had brought. The ship was registered X-401V as Cross-Foster CF-1 (serial #1) to Cross-Foster Aircraft Co. No data was offered on any of its operational history, nor its final disposition. The basis for this report was offered by Earl C. Reed, a mid-western legend who was very close to the project while it was in development. *(Photos from F. G. Freeman and Louis M. Lowry Collections.)*

CROSS-FOSTER CF-1

The Ellington retractable-wing.

For years pilots have dreamed about an airplane that could get off in a few hundred feet, climb like a heaven-bound angel, then come wafting back down with a slow landing speed. But, once in the air and off to somewhere, they also wanted to eat up the miles and go like a bat out of hell! Well sir, this type of airplane was never a reality, that is, until these two young fellows from Great Falls, Montana said it was possible. And, they could prove it too! Knowing that an airplane of this type would have to have something like variable wing area, these two (Con Ellington & Earle Hansen) studied the problem and devised a method that seemed to work. With all of the secret buried in the fuselage, the wing could be extended to its full-span limit of 32 ft. for take-off, climb-out, and landings. It could then be retracted inward to 25 ft. of span for cruise at optimum altitude; as a bonus, for more speed, they also incorporated a retractable landing gear.

This, then, as shown on the preceding page, was the "Ellington Special," a ship that Hansen had flight-tested for a year and a half with not a hitch in any of the "works" at any time. Powered with a seven cylinder LeBlond 7D engine of 90 h.p., the one-seater looked and acted pretty much like a normal airplane with its wings extended and the landing gear down. Take-offs were short, climb-out was good, top speed was about 110, and it could be landed at less than 40 m.p.h. But, once at altitude, the pilot could retract the landing gear, crank in the wing to a 25 ft. span, and top speed jumped easily to 170 m.p.h.! With a variable-pitch propeller, the performance would have been even better. You might say, that surely, the telescoping wing was not a new idea, the idea had been around for years, and several builders had tried it, but it had never really worked before. The "Ellington Special" had proven that it was possible with the right principles.

The "Special" was pretty much of normal construction except for the ribbed steel wing stub that was built into the fuselage; it was this assembly that housed the wing-retracting mechanism. The airplane flew beautifully with the wing panels extended, and went like a house-afire with the wings pulled in. This was touted as a major break-through in airplane design, and it was, but for some reason the excitement soon died and nothing ever came of the promising project. Built in 1938 in the back of a garage, the ship was duly registered as NX-19955, but it was then listed as the "Barkhoff Retractable Wing" and not as the "Ellington Special." Apparently there is more story to this tale than we came to know. *(Photos from Gerald H. Balzer Collection.)*

Back in the 1930s there was a flying-service operator in Nebraska that advertised the following slogan – **"FLY WITH US AND YOU'LL NEVER WALK AGAIN!"** Ad-men were more naive back then.

As a method of registration different from ours, foreign aircraft were marked with letters of the alphabet that identified the country they operated in. Here are some amusing examples seen over the years — **F-AANY** (French), **I-GULL** (Italy), **I-RIDE** (Italy), **G-AAWD** (British), **G-EATS** (British), **PH-IZZ** (in Holland), **I-FAKE** and **I-BIS** (both in Italy). It is probable there are and were many more that evoked a smile!

All us "old-timers" knew the so-called "depression" was really with us and upon us (1931-33) when to buy a one-dollar hop around the airport was about as easy to muster up as "moola" (money) for a world-cruise!

WACO ATO - WRIGHT J5

He flew every day for ten years!

Dr. John D. Brock of Kansas City set a record nearly 60 years ago that more than likely stands to this day. You see, he had flown at least once every day for 10 years without ever missing a day! Learning to fly in an old 1918 "Standard," young Brock really enjoyed his trips into the sky, flying as often as possible. Soon he had bought a "Waco 7", which was some improvement over the aging (OX-5 powered) "Standard," but in the Spring of 1928 he had bought a new "Waco 10." He loved to fly the "Ten" so well he spent most of his spare time in the air. After flying at least a little every day for more than a year, Dr. John got the idea that perhaps he could try for a record.

Officially, his record attempt started one day in November of 1929. He would fly every day for at least 15 minutes, and see if he could for a year. It didn't seem all that hard to do, and it was fun to look forward to. After he completed one year, the good doctor decided he would continue on, for a while. Another year had soon passed, and then another, — it became a pleasant habit. No need to stop now! He sold his lovable "Waco 10," and was now flying the fabulous Waco "Taper-Wing," a spirited airplane that made his daily flight a lot more fun. Soon his daily flights began to attract national attention — when he had finally flown 2000 consecutive days, Dr. Brock was invited to the White House where he was complimented for his endeavor.

Flying in the dead of winter was always a problem, especially around Kansas City. It could get real nasty! Dr. John Sometimes waited all day for a break in the weather to make his 15 minute flight — he never skipped a day, no matter what. Too, he always had his log-book signed off by a witness to prove he had flown the day. There was never any problem getting a witness — when the now-famous doctor came out to fly there were always plenty of onlookers and well-wishers. Being a rather well-to-do manufacturer of optics, Dr. Brock had money enough to add a "Waco Cabin" and a cozy "Monocoupe" to his stable of available airplanes; now, it wasn't so bad flying in the cold and miserable weather.

In November of 1939, Dr. John Brock, by now somewhat of a national celebrity, had completed 10 full years of consecutive daily flights. That was 3650 days when he had flown for at least 15 minutes, but usually more than that. Content that the record would stand, Brock retired from the daily ritual and his record will probably never be equalled! *(Photo from Earl C. Reed Collection.)*

CORNELIUS FREWING PARASOL - 1931

Cornelius "Frewing."

Among the several innovators who promised to improve airplane design was George Cornelius. He promised to eliminate the "dreaded stall," a phenomenon that was still feared by most pilots of ordinary airplanes. The logical approach to this problem, as Cornelis saw it, was to offer "automatic variable incidence" in the wing — a wing that would never reach the "stalling angle." The theory was fine, but putting it into practice was actually a lot more trouble than it was worth!

As the Cornelius "Frewing," the prototype was a parasol monoplane with open seating for two in tandem. The two wing-halves were fastened to a mechanism in the special center-section, and were operated by floating "tabs" that extended rearward from the trailing edge of each wing. These tabs governed the angle of incidence. The "Frewing " flew in 1931, and Cornelius felt the project was worth further study. It kept him busy for another decade or so, developing other configurations, but nothing ever came of it. It was a good idea in theory, but a mechanical nightmare in practice. *(A Grand Central Photo from Gerald H. Balzer Collection.)*

MOHAWK "REDSKIN" - WARNER 110

This Mohawk was a "Redskin."

The Mohawk "Pinto" was a scrappy little monoplane that was an eye-popper wherever it went, and usually heralded its presence with a couple of grass-cutting "buzz-jobs" down the runway to get everyone's attention! As introduced in late 1927 and early 1928, it always drew a crowd, but almost all soon shied away from it because the flying-public was not yet ready to accept such a far-out package that the "Pinto" presented. A small monoplane, especially a low-winged cantilever-winged monoplane, was hard for the people to accept as yet. Then too, the reputation of the feisty "Pinto" at hangar-flying sessions, that it was cursed with several bad habits, seemed to get worse with each telling, and that didn't help matters either. The "Pinto" didn't really deserve all this, but that's the way of things.

Mohawk Aircraft tried several other versions of basically the same design, hoping that a more diverse line-up would create more interest. A redesigned "Pinto" with more presence and with more power was offered as the "Spurwing." This version, with a more haughty stance, bordered on the true sport-plane with what was then a scintillating performance. A performance that drew smiles of appreciation and adoration, but still no orders to speak of.

The Mohawk staff were now groping, so they put a coupe-top canopy on the "Spurwing" and called it the "Redskin." Almost concurrently, even a "light twin" was in the making, which was basically a modified "Redskin" with more wing span and area, and was powered with two four cylinder air-cooled inverted Michigan "Rover" engines of some 55 h.p. each. In the altogether, this was a very unusual little airplane for this time, and it did draw some inquiries about price and availability, but its ability to fly with "one engine out" at gross load was questionable. This caused prospects to be stand-offish to say the least. So then, Mohawk now had four models to offer the market that pleased the lookie-loos, but the roster of "Mohawk" airplane owners was not a very big list!

When finally, Professor John D. Akerman, solver of aerodynamic problems, was asked to review the discouraging situation, he suggested a redesign of the basic "Pinto" to take some of the feistiness out of its character, offering the thought that not all prospective buyers would be dare-devil pilots! The new redesigned "Pinto" as certificated and introduced in 1930 was slightly larger with longer moment-arms for a more docile response and overall was a more pleasant airplane to manage. The pity of it is that Mohawk Aircraft now had an airplane the would eventually sell, but the market for this type of sporty two-seater had all but disappeared. Had the "depression" of this period in time not stifled just about everything in America, the struggling Mohawk Aircraft Co. could have survived and perhaps even prospered. Wouldn't that have been nice! *(Photos from the Roy Oberg and Gerald H. Balzer Collections.)*

The Mohawk "Twin."

The Waterman "Rubber Duck."

Waldo Waterman, was a kindly and highly visible fixture in the California aviation scene since the "Early Bird" days. He was also into everything and was certainly well known. He was manager of one of the busiest airports in Southern California, and he was a test-pilot for Bach Aircraft when they were building their line of odd-ball "Tri-Motors." He acted as consultant to just about anyone who needed help. He was that good!

Always full of ideas, he took it upon himself to form the Waterman Aircraft Syndicate to raise financing for a new design that was to be built as the "Flex-Wing." This was to be a four-Place cabin monoplane with controllable hydraulic struts supporting the wing. This contrivance allowed flexing of the wings in rough and bumpy air, thus (theoretically) absorbing the jolts and smoothing out the ride.

The "Syndicate" was formed with 25 subscribers who were solicited for a $1000 contribution each. This money was to sustain the manufacture and the development of the new airplane. Robert Porter, who was president of Kinner Motors, donated the newly developed large five cylinder Kinner C5 engine rated 190 h.p. as his contribution to the project. The airplane was completed in June of 1930 and received plenty of newsreel and press publicity because of tis oddity. Because of the new-fangled attributes promised to the public, it soon earned the name of "Rubber Duck" and it was taken to The National Air Races of 1930 (23 Aug. - Sept.), held in Chicago. Like many other airplanes, it went to the races for national exposure. It demonstrated almost every day and became a feature of the week-long show, between race events.

In theory and in practice the "Flex-Wing" system changed dihedral and also the wing's angle of incidence because the wings were hinged at a 30 degree angle to the thrust line. Thus, when the dihedral angle was changed manually, so was the angle of incidence. For landing, the wing was rigged nearly flat (span-wise) thereby offering the most angle of incidence for a slower glide and a slower touch-down. So far all this sounds good, but it actually didn't work out as planned!

One would assume that, as in theory, the wings under airload would flex against the hydraulic struts to dampen the bumps in rough air. Well, actually the wing stayed more or less in place, and the fuselage rose and fell with the rise and fall of the air currents! Needless to say, you had to have a strong stomach and a good sense of humor for this kind of flying. Some say that Waterman began calling it the "Flapper." So, what happened? The theory was good. While still on the ramp, the wing would be adjusted from the cockpit manually for the most efficient angle of dihedral and angle of incidence for take-off; then for climb out, optimum cruise, best glide, and slowest landing. Surely a good idea, but why didn't it work that way? The final disposition of this airplane is unknown, but it did become a "Hangar Queen" for a while. As the Waterman 4CLM, it was registered as X-169W (serial #1) to Waldo Waterman. But that wasn't the last you heard of "Waldo." He was full of ideas, and is now one of the memorable names in aviation history. *(Photos from Gerald H. Balzer Collection.)*

Shown on ramp in extreme angle of dihedral.

BELGIAN R.S.V. BIPLANE - 1929 - RENARD 5 CYL

Gates R.S.V. was a "convertible."

For a time during the "Lindbergh Era" (1927-29), anybody with an adventurous leaning and a fair amount of money to spend hankered to be in the "airplane business." Building airplanes, operating flying schools, mapping and air photography, and airport services; all became attractive avenues into the rosy future of the airplane-business. Even major financing was standing in line looking for a "good opportunity!"

Because aviation was expanding by leaps and bounds (relatively), those with big dreams and a little spunk scurried around to get into the action! Ivan Gates, who had operated a famous "Flying Circus" back in earlier years, saw his "circus" venture sagging, so he was shopping around for some quick way to prosper and stay in business. One of the ways to quick success, or some thought, was to look at foreign airplanes that were already a success. Or perhaps they would be easily adaptable to American tastes and needs, and could be built here in this country under license.

One such airplane was the Belgian R.S.V. (Renard-Stampe-Vertongen) convertible monoplane-biplane with a five cylinder Renard engine that apparently captivated Ivan Gates; even to the extent that he formed a company to market this airplane here in this country, under license. An average two-seater, the R.S.V. could be operated easily as a biplane, or the lower wing could be removed and the airplane then became a sporty strut-braced parasol monoplane. Either way, it took only two hours to make a change from one to the other. A listed price was $3750 for the monoplane, and $4500 for the plane with extra wings and stuff to make it into a biplane.

One never knows what it is that attracts a man to a certain airplane. Perhaps it is stance or just a feel, but in this case Ivan Gates finally learned he had made a big mistake and picked a loser. One example was sent to Gates for demonstration, and in due time it fell flat on its face. Only mild interest was generated and the venture became a flop. Research revealed perhaps three other examples of the R.S.V. in this country, but their operational history is unknown. Ivan Gates also had a hand in the Gates-Day "New Standard." The "New Standard" line as revived by Charles Day became versatile airplanes and did become a moderate success. But, in the collapse of most of the aviation industry (1931-33), it also became a casualty to the "sickness" that was spreading like a plague all over the country! In despair, Ivan Gates perhaps saw his future as grim and hopeless — he jumped out of the window of a towering Manhattan skyscraper!! *(Photos from Gerald H. Balzer Collection.)*

R.S.V. in head-on view.

The Wright-Tuttle Aircraft Motors Corp. of Anderson, Indiana, had actually negotiated first for the Belgian "Renard-Stampe-Vertongen" (R.S.V.). The scope of the deal was larger than they had cared to tackle, so they opted to manufacture and distribute the five cylinder Renard WT-5 (120 h.p.) engine, and let Ivan Gates have the airplane. Of the R.S.V. examples that were here in this country, it could not be determined which were imported and which were built here. *(Photos from Gerald H. Balzer Collection.)*

WACO 9 EXPERIMENT - 1926

Way back in the days of the "Waco 9" (1925-26), airplane designers were beginning to consider various aerodynamic "helpers" to aid pilots in keeping the airplane in trim. An aid was added early-on to ease control pressures by using balance-horns (remember the "Elephant Ears" on the early "Travel Air"), and off-set control hinges, etc. The adjustable horizontal stabilizer, to compensate for weight placed on either side of the C.G., was also coming into practice. Sometimes the workings of this assembly became complicated and required frequent maintenance.

So, somebody at "Waco" was playing around with different concepts and came up with a "foil" placed in the slipstream. As shown here, it was con-

trolled from the cockpit by cables. Different positions cranked in, either up or down, would accomplish nose-up or nose-down at the discretion of the pilot. This was to maintain level-flight despite abnormal placing of weight in the load-carrying area of the fuselage. When asked about this project years later, hardly anyone could remember it! Such is progress! *(Photos from Marion Havelaar Collection.)*

Lady Mary Heath — again.

Lady Mary Heath, British no less, was working for A.C.E. "Cirrus" engines, which were Americanized versions of the British "Cirrus" Mk. 3. She traveled about the countryside promoting these engines, which were at that time being used exclusively in the "Great Lakes" 2-T-1 sport-trainer. Shown here, she is alongside the airplane that was used as a scout-plane by Cliff Henderson for mapping out the route for the 1929 National Air Tour, also known as the Ford Air Tour. On this visit to the Great Lakes factory in Cleveland, Ohio, she was asked to fly this airplane to compare it with the Avro "Avian" she had normally been flying. The caption on the photo said: "Shortly after the photo was taken, Lady Mary had stalled it, "spun in" and crashed thru' the roof of a hangar!" There was a factory mechanic in the front cockpit and both walked away from the surely unexpected crash with barely a scratch! *(Photo from Charles W. Meyers Collection.)*

N.A.B.A. THE WONDER-PLANE - 1931

"N.A.B.A.," the wonder-plane.

Step right up ladies and gentleman to see the "N.A.B.A.," the wonder-plane! Of course, this was said very much in jest, but this was a flivver-plane that packed some innovations and features that bordered on the revolutionary for light aircraft of this time. It was perhaps one of the first lightplanes to feature a manageable "tri-cycle" landing gear; the nose-wheel was steerable and the roly-poly "air-wheels" (very low pressure) soaked up all kinds of rough going. Being so low to the ground, it was but an easy step to get into the cockpit. The large cockpit cut-out appeared to offer roomy comfort and good protection. The airplane was light enough so that one person could man-handle it on the ground with veritable ease, if need be.

The big hi-lift wing with gobs of dihedral, and the aerodynamic geometry with long moment arms were typical of lightplane design which offered gentle habits and the soul of a glider. The two cylinder engine was described as a "Peters-Conversion" of the miserable Lawrance "Twin," which wasn't a very wise selection. But, perhaps the "conversion," however done, had made it into a semblance of a genuine aircraft engine. "N.A.B.A." flew around the countryside of California for about a year or so (1931-32) and eventually suffered a forced landing up in the mountains that damaged it beyond practical repair. It was registered as X-10682 as Peters N.A.B.A. (serial #1) Converted Lawrance Twin, 2POLM, Berkeley, California. Peters had organized the National Aircraft Builders Association (NABA) in Salinas, California. Peters said their professional goal was "to make the joy of flying popular, and possible for everyone!" *(Photo from Gerald H. Balzer Collection.)*

SIMPLEX KITE MODEL S-2 - 1930 - SZEKELY SR-3-O 40 HP

The Simplex "Kite!"

Simplex Aircraft, out of Defiance, Ohio, built the jaunty "Red Arrow" mid-wing monoplanes for several years, but the line of peppy sport-planes did not do too well in sales, so they were out there only in small numbers. By 1930 things at the plant were at a near stand-still, so they were groping, as were several other airplane manufacturers, for something that would keep the thinned-out staff busy, and maybe even make a buck or two in the process.

The contrivance shown here is the Simplex "Kite." As the only photo available shows, it doesn't reveal much of its total makeup, but surely, somebody must have gone over the edge to come up with something like this! Basically, from what we can see, it would be classed as a flying-wing with a steel tube out-rigger boom to fasten the tail-group on. The occupants (they said two, no less) were huddled behind the engine installation assembly as they sat on the wing. There seems to be no inkling of construction around the seating area.

Then again, from what we can see here, perhaps it wasn't finished. But, then again, perhaps this is all there is to it! The three cylinder engine out front was a Szekely SR-3-0 of some 40 h.p. perched on a steel-tube frame with a fuel tank in behind the gear-case forming some semblance of fairing to the whole mess. The lovely cantilever wing, which looks big enough to support a much larger airplane, is the biggest part of this whole airplane. Perhaps, that is why they called it the "kite." As an ultra-light experiment, they labeled it simply as the "Model S-2," registered X-489M as serial #1. This looks like an intriguing little project, but after much effort, no other data was available. *(Photo from Gerald H. Balzer Collection.)*

BERLINER-JOYCE ALL VISION MDOEL 29-1 - 1929-30 - KINNER K5

Berliner-Joyce "All Vision."

The Berliner-Joyce Aircraft Corp. was formed in 1929 as a successor to the Berliner Aircraft Corp. that built the OX-5 powered "Berliner CM-4" parasol monoplane. This was a particularly lovely airplane that seated three, and several were built, but it didn't fare well against all the OX-5 powered bi-planes that were on the market at that time.

Henry Berliner and Temple Joyce, along with William H. Miller as chief engineer, were the nucleus of the new firm and they looked about for a place to start. Opting for a modest beginning, they chose their "Model 29-1," which as shown here, was a high-winged cabin monoplane they called "All Vision." Of the opinion that an airplane such as this would be used by happy-go-lucky weekend pilots, and those wrapped up in the serious business of learning to fly, they estimated from experience there would be scads of other airplanes in the air at the same time. It would then be of prime importance that everyone see each other! In the "29-1" All-Vision that would be easy to do because of the clear vision possible in almost any direction!

Of rather generous proportion, with sensible aerodynamic geometry, it was a carefree airplane that was a pleasure to fly. The rugged structure soaked up a lot of punishment and instilled a sense of confidence. The two-place tandem seating allowed for a slender figure, and offered plenty of leg-room. As powered with the popular five cylinder Kinner K5 engine of 100 h.p. the power was ample, but not enough to instill surges of bravado into the pilot. Everything about the "29-1" was calm and sedate, but surely, it was meant to be that way!

Temple Joyce flew the "All Vision" on its maiden flight in August of 1929, and only two months or so later the stock-market had crashed, and most of aircraft manufacturing had crashed with it! Temple Joyce, because of his earlier career as a test-pilot, had many friends in high places; his "car-salesman" aptitude helped also. The firm soon mustered up several small military contracts that held the business above water for a while. In an incorporation move, the company became B/J Aircraft, and new designs were coming out the door in bunches. But honestly, the only "Berliner-Joyce that was probably memorable to the most people was the bally-hooed P-16, a two-seated "Pursuit" (Fighter) for the U.S. Army Air Corps. Powered with the 600 h.p. (12 cylinder) vee-type Curtiss "Conqueror" engine which could bellow out the sweetest sound you ever heard!

Henry Berliner, disappointed in the turn of events, left the firm in 1930 to take a position at "ERCO," who later developed the famous two-control "Ercoupe." Before long, B/J became a pawn in stock manipulations, financial trades, and other fancy doings that only bankers and lawyers can come up with! It finally became a division of North American Aviation (backed by General Motors), and in due course, all B/J designs and projects became obsolete and useless! Lost in the shuffle of "Big Business," B/J lost all of its identity and the 29-1 "All Vision," that rolled out of the shop with such promise, is now barely a footnote in the annals of aviation history. *(Photo from North American Aviation.)*

BERLINER PARASOL CM-4 - OX-5 ENGINE

The Berliner "Parasol" of 1928.

AMERICAN EAGLE PHAETON R-540 - WRIGHT J6-5 165 HP

The American Eagle "Phaeton" as trimmed for racing!

Now, is this any way to treat a perfectly good "American Eagle?" Looks like someone chopped off about three ft. or so on each of the wings on each size, and what's left looks like hardly enough to keep it in the air! Actually, this sort of treatment was not so unusual back then in the Midwest. All summer long, just about every weekend, there were fair-dates, air-shows and air-races (regional) somewhere in neighboring states. Most of the bally-hooed programs featured pylon-races in "cubic inch class" with no apparent restrictions. So, no matter if you flew a hopped-up Heath "Parasol" or a Laird "Speedwing," chances were good that you could most always make some money to pay for the gas, or maybe win a five gallon can of "Red Crown" aviation-grade motor oil as a prize.

The "American Eagle," shown here, was originally a stock "Phaeton" powered with the five cylinder Wright J6-5 (R-540) engine of 165 h.p., and outside of the severely clipped wings, no other outlandish aids to speed are visible. Incidentally, this same ship was used as a "company hack" and it was asked to do many unusual things. Here the two-seated front cockpit was faired over to close that gaping hole, but this was an option offered even on the standard model. The standard production model (R-540) "Phaeton" was not exactly a raving beauty, but as butchered in this photo, it's enough to make one shake his head and turn away in sadness. *(Photo from Louis M. "Tex" Lowry Collection.)*

The Eyerly "Whiffle Hen."

As some have often said about Lee Eyerly of the Eyerly School of Aeronautics, he always kept the students busy learning, and well immersed in projects that reflected the mood and the progression of the times. An earlier design by the Eyerly School was the neat little "Lee Monoplane," also featured in this book (see page 19). A couple of years later after the "Lee Mono" project, it is assumed that the "Aeronautical School' was still operating profitably, and a younger batch of students were hard at work on a more up-to-date project.

The project as it rolled out in mid-1931, was the cute-as-a-bug's ear "Whiffle Hen." As shown here, its design was influenced by newer ideas and the burgeoning lightplane movement. Whereas many of the other school-built lightplane designs with low-power engines were just a little more than powered gliders. Now, this here "Wiffle Hen," tho' light and small, was pretty much a genuine airplane. Powered with the forty-horse Continental A-40 engine, it seated two side-by-side in closed-in comfort. Lacking any performance data, it would be safe to say that this little "Whiffle" was at least as good as any other airplane of this type.

Years later, there was talk going around among the hangar-fliers about an "Ol' Taylorcraft" up in the hangar-rafters at the airport in Hillsboro, Oregon. Well, wouldn't 'cha know it, it turned out to be the Eyerly "Whiffle Hen" of 1931! We're talkin' about the mid-1970s; perhaps it is there yet! *(Photo from Gerald H. Balzer Collection.)*

The Wallace "Touroplane" all folded up. (Smithsonian.)

The folding-wing feature, for one reason or another, was thought to be quite important in early days of airplane operation. But then, as it later turned out, it just never proved to be useful enough to warrant the added hardware and, of course, the added expense. At least not here in the U.S.A. where space was never at a premium.

Altho' of controversial value, there were times when the folding-wing feature was actually an asset. 'Twas said a Fairchild FC-2 monoplane, back in 1928, was forced down because of engine failure in a tiny little hay-field; a field so tiny there was no possibility of ever taking off from it! So, the Fairchild's wings were folded back and the airplane, after being repaired and run up, was towed out of this little field and taxied further down the road to a larger field more suitable for a safe take-off.

Folding wings were advantageous, too, in the north-country of the U.S.A. and Canada, especially in the winter-time when a plane had to be hurriedly put under cover due to an approaching storm. Most of the "folders" were designed to be operated by one or two men without tools in a matter of minutes. This, without disconnecting any of the fuel lines, control cables or control rods, and could be erected just as easily without losing any of the alignment in the rigging.

This feature was offered on both monoplanes and biplanes, usually to a folded width of 10 to 14 ft., or about the width of the average one-car garage. Nearly all of them could be secured well enough in the folded position to allow towing over average roads to and from the airport. The folding wing feature finally fizzled out in this country, but had much greater acceptance for a longer time in other places around the world.

Now and then, one can still see this feature brought back into use on certain designs in the home-built movement where amateur designers and builders have a broader choice to specialize and to experiment. Being able to fold the wings back for space-saving storage was always more or less a gimmick, but there have been stories galore of the young flying-enthusiast who kept his plane at home in the carport, and towed it to the local airport for a weekend of flying.

American Eagle A-429 folded up. (Smithsonian)

Buhl-Verville "Airster" folded. (Alfred V. Verville)

TAYLOR E-2 CUB - 1930 - SALMSON AD-9 40 HP

This "Cub" was a great, great, great, Grandma!

Almost everyone will surely spot this little airplane as a "Cub," a basic design that has been unspoiled by the passage of time, and very little affected by the relentless sweep of so-called progress. Also, nearly everyone has been exposed too, to the fantastic lore of the "Cub" in some way or another. So then, it is hardly necessary to say that literally thousands of pilots had earned their wings in the "Cub," or that it has done just about everything that a low-powered airplane can do!

What should be said here is that you are now looking at the great-great-great Grandmother of all the little "Cubs." Yes, the very first airplane of this type. Shown here, she poses demurely at her rather inconspicuous debut back in 1930. Standing almost skeptically with folded arms in front of her is the young fellow who conceived her — one C. Gilbert Taylor. It would be fantasy to say that he could foresee the gravity of this occasion, or what a memorable day this would be in the annals of light airplane development. The mannerly fellow in right foreground was the pilot who got to fly mademoiselle "Cub" while she tried out her wings for the first time. A smug little character, no doubt she smiled happily to herself as she was nudged around by the playful airstream, thinking perhaps this flying business was actually quite a snap, and rather interesting after all.

Tried with several different small airplane engines in her earlier development, the prototype "Cub" is shown here with the little nine cylinder radial Salmson AD-9 (French) engine of 40 h.p., the one that first made her fly. Being of foreign manufacture, its use in a plane slated for quantity production was considered risky. Installation of the brand-new (four cylinder) flat-four

Continental A-40 engine of 37 h.p. was found to be more practical. This combination was developed into the model E-2. First approved for manufacture in June of 1931, the "Cub," as built then by the Taylor Aircraft Corp. of Bradford, Pa., was not an immediate hit, but it did stir up considerable interest, and sales gradually increased as time went on. Selling for $1325 in 1931, and offering reliability with best possible economy, the "Cub" E-2 was a real bargain. Succeeding where most others failed, it went on to sell, and sell. By 1935, it was a rare airport indeed that didn't harbor at least one or two Taylor "Cubs." Built in two other companion-models, known as the F-2 and H-2, the E-2 was finally discontinued late in 1935 to make way for the new J-2. Shortly after, the Taylor "Cub" became the Piper "Cub," but that's another story. Little did that first "Cub" know that she would be followed with so many of her own kind!! *(Photo from Gerald H. Balzer Collection.)*

AMERICAN EAGLE A-429 - LE BLOND 60

American Eagle A-429

In the frenzied rush to cash in on a literal bonus, and to have something for everybody, "American Eagle" offered a lineup for 1929 that bordered on the ridiculous. Among these was a cute little sport biplane that looked like it had been brought from somewhere out of the past. Well, in fact it was. What "American Eagle" called the model A-429 was actually a modified copy of the Longren "Sport" of 1925! Powered with the five cylinder LeBlond 60, the A-429 used the familiar "Longren" wings, which could be folded, the landing gear was updated, and the fuselage was of welded steel tubes instead of molded wood and fiber. It was a nice little ship, and had many things to its credit, but it got lost somewhere in the shuffle. *(Photo from Gerald H. Balzer Collection.)*